Forever Wormingford

ALSO BY RONALD BLYTHE

The Wormingford Series

Word from Wormingford
Out of the Valley
Borderland
A Year at Bottengoms Farm
The Bookman's Tale River Diary
Village Hours
Under a Broad Sky
In the Artist's Garden
Forever Wormingford

Fiction
A Treasonable Growth
Immediate Possession
The Short Stories of Ronald Blythe
The Assassin

Non-Fiction
The Age of Illusion
William Hazlitt: Selected Writings
Akenfield
The View in Winter
Writing in a War
Places: An Anthology of Britain
From the Headlands
Divine Landscapes
Private Words
Aldeburgh Anthology

FOREVER WORMINGFORD

RONALD BLYTHE

CANTERBURY
PRESS
Norwich

© Ronald Blythe 2017
First published in 2017 by the Canterbury Press Norwich
Editorial office
3rd Floor, Invicta House
108–114 Golden Lane
London EC1Y 0TG, UK
www.canterburypress.co.uk

Canterbury Press is an imprint of Hymns Ancient & Modern Ltd
(a registered charity)

Hymns Ancient & Modern® is a registered trademark of
Hymns Ancient & Modern Ltd
13A Hellesdon Park Road, Norwich,
Norfolk NR6 5DR, UK

All rights reserved. No part of this publication may be reproduced,
stored in a retrieval system, or transmitted,
in any form or by any means, electronic, mechanical,
photocopying or otherwise, without the prior permission of
the publisher, Canterbury Press.

The Author has asserted his right under the Copyright, Designs and
Patents Act 1988 to be identified as the Author of this Work

British Library Cataloguing in Publication data

A catalogue record for this book is available
from the British Library

978 1 78622 027 1

Typeset by Manila Typesetting Company
Printed and bound in Great Britain by
CPI Group (UK) Ltd

CONTENTS

January
New Year's Eve	1
Grand Company	3
The Akenfield Chair	5
Painters and Trees	7
Twelfth Night	9
George Herbert on the BBC	11
The Enlightened One	13
Interiors	14
The Incumbents' Board	16
The Lay Canon	18

February
Prisoners' Lessons	21
On the Road with St Paul	23
The Lengthening of the Light	25
Midwinter Spring	27

March
Stony Ground	29
Window Songs	31
A Writer Must Always Have Something to Say	33
At Blythburgh	35
The Unsheltered	36

Alice in Oxford 38
Teachers 40

April
Mrs Fox's Fritillary Field 43
The Lady Julian 45
Digging 47
Cleaning Winter off the Windows 49
My Trees 51
East Anglian Masters 53
Jane Austen in Church 55

May
Cuckoo 57
Shepherd Sunday 59
Old Ladies 61
The Reverend Francis Kilvert 63
The Great Barge 65
The Mesolithic Axe 67
Calling the Banns 69
George Herbert's First Sermon 71
Ascension Day 73

June
What Is a Hymn? 76
Grass 77
St Barnabas 79
Mount Bures 81
Scything the Rough 83

Forever Wormingford

July

High Summer	86
The Prayer Book Society Arrives	88
The Curate Is Confirmed	90
Such Good Things	92
The Pilgrimage to Helpston	94
St Edmundsbury Cathedral	96

August

John Bottengoms, 1375	98
Church Lavatories and Early English Windows	100
Our Flower-Show	102
Jonathan Mends the Track	104
Feet	106
The Aftermath	108

September

To Discoed	111
The Least of the Apostles	113
Applause	115
The Potter	117
Lancelot Andrewes	119
The Freshness of Repeated Actions	121
Liturgy	123
Quarter Day	125

October

John Betjeman's Felixstowe	128
Colchester Boy	130

Forever Wormingford

Michaelmas Wakes	132
Weather	134
St Luke – Renaissance Man	136
Tobit and Late Roses	138
'Only Luke Is with Me'	140

November

Paraclete	142
Kneelers	144
Ash before Oak	146
George Herbert and the Backs	148

December

St Edmund's Day	151
The Unremembered Ones	153
School Bus	155
Poverty	157
The Holly Hedge	159
Carols	162
Christmas in Cornwall	164

JANUARY

New Year's Eve

JOACHIM, the Jewish doctor from the Berlin synagogue, kindly drives me to the Midnight, and is transfixed by Wormingford Church, a medieval stone lantern whose fretted brilliance glitters over the parked cars.

Back at the old farmhouse, his Hanukkah candles will waver in the window as part of the Festival of Lights, which celebrates the rededication of the Temple by Judas Maccabaeus in 165 BC. Every morning, Joachim goes up to his room and prays for one hour, facing east. Prayer is an art that has to be practised. 'Let us pray,' I quietly invite the congregation. I read wonderful words.

Now, on New Year's Eve, the guests gone, I find a pearl of candle wax on the windowsill, and leave it there. Jews would seem to be more obedient to Christ's prayer-rules than his own followers. This is how Canon Andrew Linzey sums up these rules, in his little book *The Sayings of Jesus*. I often read them, and if I obey them in some measure that falls short of Joachim's whole hour of daily prayer, it is because my writer's mind tends to fly about, alighting on this and that, like one of my August dragonflies from the pond. Anyway, this is what Andrew says.

'Jesus gives little advice about prayer except that it should be unhypocritical, devoid of empty phrases, and preferably done in secret (Matthew 6.1–8; Mark 12.38, 40). The public

Forever Wormingford

prayers and self-regarding rituals of the scribes and Pharisees are treated with scorn (Matthew 6.16–18). The prayer recommended by Jesus is simple and almost entirely petitionary in character (Matthew 6.9–13). His own prayer takes place before or after public ministry; he withdraws to pray and almost always prays alone. In John's Gospel, he prays that his disciples may be kept in the truth, protected from evil, and "may all be one . . . so that the world may believe".'

Prayer, for Teilhard de Chardin, was 'to lose oneself in the unfathomable' – he was talking of adoration. For George Herbert, it was the best kind of conversation he could find on earth. Sickly, tramping to Salisbury Cathedral through the water-meadows, or mounted on his horse on the heights of Wiltshire, he would pray, or rather talk:

> Come, my Light, my Feast, my Strength;
> Such a Light as shows a Feast,
> Such a Feast as mends in length,
> Such a Strength as makes his guest.

Having broken through prayer into conversation with Christ, Herbert was already half in heaven – as slow-dying people often are – and he could not thank prayer enough for giving him such carefree access. So he wrote his happy extravaganza, which is a kind of Jacobean court eulogy addressed to the highest favour that can be awarded to a subject.

Witty, over the top, bursting with gratitude for its giving him such divine access to 'my Friend', he can be playful and profound all at once. 'Of what an easie quick Access, My blessed Lord art thou!' And then – the famous fun. What is prayer?

Forever Wormingford

It is:

Church-bels beyond the starrs heard, the souls bloud,
The land of spices; something understood.

Grand Company

THE Epiphany, the time for poets. Wild journeys, travelling light, destination, great gifts. And roses still in bloom. The white cat sleeping it off – the non-existent winter. The cards have tumbled down; the wreckage of an iced cake calls for appetite; the bottles wink. Two funerals: a lad of 19, and Bobby the lorry driver, in his eighties.

Leading the procession to Bobby's grave, I am anxious not to tread on the daffodil shoots. The gravedigger with windblown curls takes the shine off his spade with a bit of sackcloth. All is as it should be – except for teenage Matthew. Fat blackbirds hop about in the bare hedges.

Colin brings his little boy to see me, plus their happy dog. Both – the boy and the dog, that is – make a beeline for the stairs. We hear them crashing about in the ancient rooms. For some reason unknown to me, there is always this rush to the top of the house.

The boy is half Belgian, and chatters in a flood of two languages. Colin is half Scottish; I am most Suffolk. Colin's chickens are so free-range that we have to slow down so as not to slaughter them as we drive to church.

Having a moment to spare, I visit the monuments. These are amazing. Proustian. Such obsequies! Not a bit like those that I perform for Bobby. Although he was lowered in to

Forever Wormingford

depths of fine language; for we are 'not to be sorry as men without hope . . .'

Waiting for Sunday lunch with the neighbours, I enter the glorious world of the Little Horkesley dead. First, there is Richard Knight, a relation of the Thomas Knight who, in 1783, adopted Jane Austen's father, Edward, and whose excellent character was given to Mr Knightley in *Emma*. Serving at the altar, my feet are firmly placed on the riven memorial to one who set the standard for a gentleman.

Startlingly, by the entrance to the church lie three enormous wooden people. These are the de Horkesleys, no less: Robert, William, and Emma. And then, further inside, is the battered brass of the Mayor of Bordeaux and captain of Fronsac, in Guinne. We sing evensong in great company.

What dust these fine folk left was blown to the winds on 21 September 1940, when a German parachute-mine fell into the church, fragmenting its past. No one was killed or injured. Everything disappeared, then returned in a later guise. And Major-General de Havilland – Olivia's cousin –who lived at the Hall, insisted that what had vanished must be replicated. Our little parish contains the plots of a dozen blockbusters. They sing well there, too.

Climbing the pulpit, I say: 'When we open a door, a box, or ourselves, what lies inside becomes manifest. Something that was hidden shows itself.' For centuries, the prophets have spoken of a spiritual force that would stay hidden until it would manifest itself in a newborn child, in a precocious boy, in a poor homeless young man, in a welcome guest at Bethany, in a marvellous storyteller, in the Christ.

Forever Wormingford

But it is three very grand people who arrive at the Epiphany: King Gaspar, King Melchior, and King Balthasar – monarchs you will not find in scripture.

The Akenfield Chair

A SEPIA, half-lit day. Wild duck fly over, squawking and honking. I am desultory: reading a bit of this, writing a bit of that. I could have gardened, I tell myself. The white cat is a blur against the window.

On Sunday, Christ is being presented at the Temple. He is 40 days old. They used to call it 'the Meeting', i.e. of the child with aged Simeon. They used to sing *Lumen ad revelationem*. Not much *lumen* on the ancient farm at this moment, but always plenty of revelation.

A friend has brought me the Akenfield chair, a mighty piece of furniture, lugging it through the wet garden. It is made of various woods from the trees where I used to live. Tim made it, and Jason set it down on the brick floor, where it at once became part of the old house. It is pale and heavy, and very hard. Could it bear a cushion? Its puritan beauty might flinch from such indulgence.

Jason returns to his old farmhouse, where he is a wonderful drawer of animals. Portraits of his ewes and cows look down on us in the pub. Furniture-makers used to be called joiners. I must not place the new chair near a radiator, or else what Tim has joined together will come apart.

I observe it lovingly after he has driven away, thinking of how it will outlive me, how it will fade and become worn, how a woman will call her husband to move it. It has a small drawer at the back in which I have put a card which says: 'Tim Whiting made me, 2014.'

The Suffolk poet Robert Bloomfield honoured his gate-legged table with a poem. I see him bent over it, pushing his pen. He is the first writer I ever wrote about – this when I was 15. His famous work was *The Farmer's Boy*, a Georgian idyll, a blissful view of life on the land, shorn of its hardships. He received a fortune for it, but died penniless.

His long poem became an agricultural party-piece. Young men would stand up in the pub and spout it by the yard. Or sing it. There were singing pubs and non-singing pubs. Vaughan Williams, collecting folk-songs before the First World War, asked a young man to sing him a song so that he could write it down, but they were both thrown out of the bar by the landlord because it wasn't a singing pub.

Now and then, I take a non-singing funeral. 'Immortal, Invisible', I announced the other day. A full church, but hardly a sound. I could hardly say, 'Sing up!' with the coffin in front of me.

Various reasons are given for these packed non-singing funerals. Some say that the abolition of school assemblies has produced a hymnless population. Gareth is doing his best, of course. But what a loss. No 'Immortal, Invisible, God only wise' – yet Nine Lessons and Carols only a month ago, and in full voice.

But tears. Such tears from those who had not expected to cry. Usually the mourners are worn out with hospitals and drugs, with the ferocity of loss. The practice of religion brings philosophy as well as faith. All these things fill the wide spaces of an old country church for a funeral. The congregation is perfectly sad. 'And afterwards at the White Horse.' And afterwards the expense – £10,000, they reckon.

But enough of these wintry thoughts. A woman mounts the Temple steps. She is holding a child.

Painters and Trees

THE last time trees were given free range throughout the Royal Academy was when it honoured John Nash with a retrospective, in the late '60s. He was the same age as David Hockney. His trees flourished in their modest fashion from Cornwall to Skye. But their roots, as it were, grew in Nash's homeland, Buckinghamshire. And particularly on the Chilterns and around the Aylesbury Plain.

As with Hockney, Nash carried the viewer into scenes of personal happiness – joy, even. It was a similar emotion to that experienced by being carried away by one of those marvellous watercolour posters on a '30s railway-station platform. One knows that young people and old places cannot be as perfect as this, and yet the entire world is transfigured simply by looking at them.

Hockney, of course, is trailing his coat before the conceptionalists, the anti-smoking lobby, the painting-versus-photography argument, if this still exists, and anything that stands in the way of simple happiness.

His Yorkshire wold – German *Wald*, forest – is but a wooded lane, which he drives from Bridlington to look at obsessively time and time again, with a carload of hi-tech aids. He is no primitive, no Alfred Wallis. Yet he creates

Forever Wormingford

traditional landscapes out of the most ordinary sights and the most sophisticated materials, and allows this unidentifiable joy of his to flood them.

Even his camera – the last word, we can be sure – is made to produce the wonder of a Box Brownie snap. His plants, including his trees, are essentially unbotanical. They conduct light and shade, leaf and hibernate, and are determinedly ordinary. They are what we miss when we are driving, not walking or staring, and were the subject-matter of Georgian poetry.

Visitors to this huge picture show will slow up by some verge, ditch, field, copse, and reconsider the purpose of their own existence. Or just to take a good look. The art critics could be thrown as they back-pedal. First California, and now this track.

I have lived most of my days under Gainsborough's and Constable's trees, and not figuratively; for many of them go on growing. Cornard Wood is just over the hill, as is Tendring Park. And I have sat beside John Nash as he sketched in the Stour Valley, and watched the willows in winter appearing on the sheet. Cigarette ash, too.

One of these crashed down in the recent gale, opening up sky and land. At night, I listen to the ashes groaning. 'That'll fall on you one of these days.' I doubt it. But it misses being a model. It is asking for attention and creaking: 'Look at me!' Hockney's wayside trees will be ill at ease in Piccadilly. But then so should we, now and then. Our joy should be elsewhere, maybe. Visionaries might be able to tell us, or an art exhibition – though no longer a station poster.

I tell another David about the tumbled willow, and he says: 'I'll bring my chainsaw.' Snowdrops are flooding where it has let in the light. You would hardly believe it was January. Paul Nash was given a camera in 1930, and photographed one of his significant images – *Monster Field.*

Twelfth Night

LONG ago, walking home, I was tempted to visit the poet Edward FitzGerald's grave on a winter's afternoon, just when the light was 'going', as we used to say. A young airman from the USAAF base with a little son in his arms was fumbling his way into the church. 'Where is the light?' he asked. Memorials glimmered all around. Light was taking its daily absence.

Since it is Twelfth Night, I take down the holly. Log fires have dulled its gloss. Crisped to a turn, it hisses from the beams to the bricks. The white cat has done for the Christmas cards. No sooner do I stand them up than she mows them down, believing this to be her duty.

I shove crushed wrapping-paper into a sack unceremoniously, empty ashes, and remove wizened apples, when, without warning, an Epiphany sun blazes in, making the ancient interior look trashy and in need of a good putting-to-rights. But, as children, we took down the paper chains and folded up the paper bells with sadness. We watched the snowman drip into nothing, and witnessed his dying. Everything was different then, as it was bound to be.

The farmhouse was in 'full Christmas' when William Shakespeare wrote *Twelfth Night* to entertain King James at Whitehall. Food-wise, what could be salted away was preserved for the bitter months ahead. The winter's cold could be terrible. You had to clutch at health for all you were worth. You could become low.

Forever Wormingford

'Keep good fires,' the Revd Sydney Smith advised a depressed friend. 'Winter wild, and winter drear Surely wintertime is here,' we sang in the village school. But in church we sang, 'Brightest and best of the sons of the morning'. Reginald Heber wrote this entrancing Epiphany hymn after discovering the *Olney Hymns*. He was so youthful, and, alas, so vulnerable to the destructive Indian heat. He listened to his hymn being sung in a Raj church below the Himalayas. It is exotic, and a far cry from Cowper's pleading 'Heal us, Emmanuel'.

Many old country people called Twelfth Night 'the real Christmas'. It was also a trickster time, when boys became girls and bonfires from the old gods challenged the light of Christ. When ice and snow made it impossible to work, play took over. See a typical Dutch winterscape: as it is far colder inside, everyone is outside, skating, running, drinking, shouting. In freezing Victorian classrooms, the children would be told to stand up and 'beat your arms' to get the circulation going. One reason for our present post-Twelfth Night aches is that our blood barely circulates. Families dine on sofas, not at tables. But then the Three Kings probably dined on a carpet.

I could pick a bunch of primroses. Not that I will; for their open presence near the house must not be disturbed. But here they are, about a dozen of them, in the Epiphany sunshine, forerunners of thousands. The sodden oak-leaves of the rains are dry and conversational. The sky is a goldmine. Lots of mud about. The church smells of pine needles and wax, and damp uncollected cards. I am to lay at Christ's feet my 'burden of carefulness'. I know exactly what the writer is getting at. So should we all.

Forever Wormingford
George Herbert on the BBC

IT IS one of those not uncommon April-in-January mornings. Cirrus clouds rinsed with gold, animals wearing haloes – which they should, of course. The white cat, spread out on a radiator below the window, like a Roman at dinner, invites the winter sun to warm her. Birds idle above.

A long time ago, standing in the school playground and looking up, I heard a little boy say: 'They don't know it's Thursday.' Now and then, I don't know it's the 14th, or whatever. Someone knocks and says: 'You are expecting me, aren't you?' 'Yes, yes, of course, come in.' I reach for the coffee/tea.

Jason has brought the Akenfield chair, a handsome descendant of the Arts and Crafts movement. It takes up its position in the ancient room with aplomb. I sit in it, and am at once enthroned. Tim, the wonderful craftsman, has made it out of oak, and maybe fruit woods. I must ask him. I sit in it apologetically, like the unworthy inheritor of a crown. It had pride of place at the Alde Festival.

The River Alde flows vaguely towards the Aldeburgh marshes, and thus to the North Sea. I lived by it when I was young. Now I live by the Stour, and in fine company: Thomas Gainsborough and John Constable. Slightly in flood, it glitters through my bedroom window.

When I was young, it poured through the low-lying cottages at Burs, just down the road. No electrics and fitted carpets in those days; so the wooden furniture was hauled up the narrow stairs until the water went down, and was swept out. Seeing today's flood victims in Gloucestershire, my heart goes out to them. Water right up to the telly, boats outside, belated insurance, no dove to announce God's forgiveness.

Constable loved rainbows. He painted one above Stoke by Nayland a few miles from here – knew how to merge the seven colours, all in their prismatic order. There could be a rainbow today, I think.

The Epiphany continues another showing. Another 'Brightest and best of the sons of the morning', among which count me. I'm not very bright in the evenings. 'Wake up, that boy at the back there!' Fragments of old protests try to stir me into action. What a hope.

On Sunday mornings, before Meriel or Mike arrives to drive me to church, I listen to the radio service, unreasonably disappointed by the thin singing, longing for that glorious full congregational sound. A priest overcomes all the techniques of broadcasting with her prayerfulness. It is very beautiful. I read George Herbert on this programme, and my friend Canon Judy Rees officiated.

I was with my friend Vikram Seth, a Hindu who comes to evensong. It was at Bemerton, near Salisbury, where Herbert was rector for a little more than two years – and changed the face of the Church of England. Should you go there, you will hear the bell that he tolled, and open the door that he opened – and not only to his parish church, but to aspects of believing which remain transforming. He was tall, young, and ill. Coughing, singing to his lute. Writing poems that no one knew about. Vikram Seth has absorbed them, even continued them.

At the Epiphany, we continue in the light. What would we see without it?

Forever Wormingford
The Enlightened One

KEITH the builder works on the old farmhouse with a kind of inherited understanding of its materials and structure. A lath-and-plaster wall is taken back to its fundamentals. Anything later than, say, 1660 is swept away by what seems to me a hand that itself is contemporaneous with this date. But I do not enquire. I watch. His 'history' and my history are unable to speak to each other.

Dust of ages fills the room. Yet the white cat remains white. Bodging falls to the floor. Keith neither swears at the work of these crude menders, nor honours what remains of the art of the Tudor builders as he frees the laths from pale crumbling daub.

The laths were made from flat strips of riven oak or beech which, when freed from the collapsed daub, are as good as new. Other parts of the house were constructed with a basketwork of willow sticks and grass. Electrical fittings are johnny-come-lately threads. Keith allows them all, somewhat alarmingly, to hang out.

At one o'clock, he stops working, and I stop watching, and we have a glass of port. After he has gone home, I pore over the wall as one might pore over an old painting, tracing its outline, its prickle of little handmade nails, its wooden Meccano of beams, seeing both its fragility and its lasting strength. The next day, Keith re-lays the brick floor, a modern addition circa 1750.

Where do natural craftsmen get their eye? Why haven't I got an eye? Keith's tools, scores of them, lie like treasure in the box that was given to him when he was 16. There cannot be many houses hereabouts where its contents haven't come in handy. Beside the tools, there are 'finds', such as a scrap of blacksmith's work: 'That'll come in handy.'

The weather being springlike, I garden. The birds sing. I find a way to get dead leaves out of the yuccas without being pierced. I dig up a dead rose, Duchess of somewhere or other, and plant a new one, a Christmas present, in its place. Though not exactly in its place; for this is something one must not do.

Taking an Epiphany matins at Little Horkesley, I tell them the story of the conversion of Buddha, the Enlightened One. I have told it to them before, but it bears repeating.

An Indian prince, youthful and beautiful, is driven in his carriage beyond his palace and its gardens for the first time. He has never seen ageing, illness . . . Such things had been kept from him. He sees a shaven-headed man in a simple yellow robe, and is told: 'He is what is called a wanderer, my Lord. Someone who has gone forth.'

'What is that – to have gone forth?'

'It means to lead a holy life, my Lord; one which is filled only with good actions, harmlessness, and kindness.'

The Buddha alighted. 'I will go forth.'

Which, after the upset at his local synagogue, is what Jesus did; what both he and the Buddha, and countless of their followers, did, carrying light wherever they went. If you follow a star, you have to look up. Epiphany should be when we see God plainly, when we walk in the light.

Interiors

THE Epiphany continues. Today, snow-light. White-blue hills, sagging boughs. A cold to take one's breath away. Delectable soups on the go. Twenty hardy ramblers descend into the valley. Keith, our Admirable Crichton, descends on me to paint a room – white. And Peter, equally versatile, thinks nothing of driving from Thetford to re-lay the brick floor.

Between them, they expose wonderful and dreadful things, a century or more of lost treasures and dirt too horrible to tell you about. For such is an ancient house: a container of modest antiquities and a lot of rubbish. Here is a George V envelope; here are objects I've been searching for since last winter. And, of course, the rooms being upside down, Paul has arrived, so cups of dusty tea.

A ramblers' club appears on the horizon, clumping its boots and beating its arms. The white cat eats a lot, and travels from radiator to radiator. I walk in the powdery orchard. I put up green woodpeckers, and hasten the squirrel on its way. Will it last? This void of winter?

I think of Georgian families in their box pews and their feet in nice clean straw as the frozen parson held forth. And singing maybe 'Turn us again, O God, show the light of thy countenance and we shall be whole', very slowly, as they did then.

I work on some poems for a composer to set. Three or four. I listen to Schubert's sad-grim *Earl King* from Wigmore Hall, supper on one knee and cat on the other, and listen to the creaky night-time winter. There are hellebores beneath the snow. They bloom on, untouched by cold. Although, pity the poor traveller on a night like this.

I remember the pre-central-heating days of my boyhood, when we baked at the front and froze at the back. Put on another jersey! Think of the homeless! I lie awake, thinking of my million snowdrops and of the owls over the river. I

Forever Wormingford

think: where have I put the breadknife? All sorts of things. Spring cleaning in January is very disturbing. And the dust! I look like a wraith.

Today, a friend flies to Ethiopia to study Coptic manuscripts, but before he did this, he drove a few miles to see Copford Church, there to see the painted *Christ in Judgement*, who is in darkness until one presses a coin into a pay slot – as one does in the high-rise car park. Then he appears, no gentle Jesus, but someone to bring one to one's knees. There can be no guilty plea. Go to Copford Church near Colchester with some small change. Be awed. This is less a pilgrimage than Addis Ababa, and on flat fields, not 8000 feet in the air.

Christmas is a hundred years past. It is what happens in January. But the Epiphany is timelessly going on and on. This is what happens to light. Ice and snow appeared in the morning, but the stream ran fast, cold, and clear. The dawn was lurid, streaking across Duncan's barn in the best Rothko style. I filled two pails from the stream, just in case of a freeze-up. The sun is hot on my back as I write. A window pane makes winter luxurious. Frozen roses scratch the glass, tight petal-spheres which will never open. To have got so far.

Well, says the neighbour, there's nothing we can do about it. He means winter.

The Incumbents' Board

I WAS about to describe what happens to me when I drift into imaginative notions about the incumbents board in church, when someone on the radio, talking about his introduction to music as a choirboy, called an old church 'a resonant chamber'.

Forever Wormingford

But I was wondering how these men preached rather than how they sang. Their flock stood around looking up. The old, sick, or pregnant sat on a ledge – 'the weakest go to the wall'. The Church Fathers – Jerome, Cyril, etc. – had their portraits painted on panels below the pulpit to remind the priests to stay orthodox and not to go off into flights of fancy. The mostly illiterate listeners hoped for a good story.

After the Reformation, the sacraments were short and the sermon was very long indeed. But, by then, listeners were able to sit, or even doze off for a bit. There might be glorious oratory, plain ignorance, inspired teaching, or just his reverence going on and on. It was a kind of rest, anyway, after a week in the fields. Chestnuts abounded.

After a hellfire sermon, the parson was shocked to see one old soul grinning. 'But Mrs Smith, you could not have been listening to what I had to say.'

'Well, sir, what I say is, let them that has 'em gnash 'em.'

What I hear when I gaze at our incumbents – those who had obtained possession of a benefice and therefore who could say more or less anything they liked as long as they said something – is the creation of the English language: Saxon words eventually holding their own against the French, Latin becoming 'learned', and our East Anglian dialect in full swing. All this talk, in the same room, for close on 1000 years.

The speakers have beautiful names. At first, a baptismal name and the name of their origins, then Christian and family names, then names followed by Oxford and Cambridge degrees, then squirearchical names for a couple of centuries, and, eventually, the names of the half-dozen vicars I actually heard and whose voices – rather than whose sermons, I must confess – I can still hear, and this with affection.

Forever Wormingford

The incumbents board is a book of life. 'I was here.' 'I spoke.' Did they speak like Chaucer, or George Herbert, or like Mr Collins, or like a saint? Or, best of all, like a poet for Christ? Who can tell.

The damp northern wall and the sun-baked south wall, the Victorian plaques, the fragmented glass from unreformed times, the Tudor and Georgian bells, the dead on the war memorial, the wafer-thin lip of the chalice, sipped for centuries, are silent.

It is left to non-believing and part-believing listeners, such as John Betjeman and Philip Larkin, to tell us what was said here; for all ancient parish churches are sound-boxes. Liturgy and local words are locked up in them; the sayings of Jesus, and sayings from the vicarage, scholarly erudition, and tales out of school. Last May, before we walked to Little Gidding, I preached at Leighton Bromswold from the wrong pulpit. Maybe only George Herbert could have got away with furnishing a church with two pulpits – one for the sermon, and one for prayer. Pale and massive they are, with huge hinges from the blacksmith, and creaking steps.

He never saw them, and we have never read his sermons. Yet I hear him, and all the great Christian writers, in our and every old nave. More now than ever.

The Lay Canon

THE autocratic nature of a great frost – it imposes its will on the winter itself. I am aware of this before I draw the curtains. Below the old farmhouse, the Stour Valley has hardened and whitened at its command, and become another place. Not a sound, not a hint of what existed before the frost.

Forever Wormingford

Flowers bloom – a flood of snowdrops and a splash of primroses, plus some final roses – but do so at attention. The horses have gone in from the cold, and the walkers have come out, their arms swinging and their talk carried by the clarity of the cold.

A dear neighbour gives a party. It is her 100th birthday, and a card from the Queen is pinned up in the Victorian schoolroom where we used to hold our PCCs and every other village parliament, the famous Wormingford flower show, and every other social get-together. We drink champagne and sing, see little difference in ourselves, wonder who the children are, and feel a kind of parochial love for each other.

A stranger, seeing my name on the church noticeboard, says that he has never heard of a lay canon. I think of the canons of my youth, who wore little rosettes on their big black hats, and of bishops in gaiters. Those were the days! The day darkens, and we bump our way home over the sleeping policemen who stop us racing up the track.

Neighbours, hurt by time, rotate in my head. And, of course, we all wish that Gordon had been with us; for, although he has been dead these many winters, it somehow does not seem right for him to be absent. Towards the end, he became worried about recognition in heaven – how a handful of particular people, including his wife, would 'see' each other there.

Epiphany is the 'seeing time', of course. And, of course, 'In the heavenly country bright Need they no created light.' So I preach somewhat poetically on this lustrous theme.

I think of poor young Reginald Heber, who, the Church of England insisted, should convert India, when, like certain

Forever Wormingford

priests, ancient and modern, he would much rather have lived out his ministry in a country parish.

My mother loved missionaries. Her lifelong example was Sister Joan, who taught our faith in Ceylon. The women she converted made my christening robe. When, in old age, Mother sailed to Australia, and the ship called at Ceylon, it was like stepping on to a holy land. She bought a small brass bell for me there.

It shares a window ledge with a Stone Age tool I found on the high ground of Wormingford, and a splinter of medieval glass from the bombing of Julian of Norwich's chapel in Norwich. Faith is often fragmentary. So, in a sense, is farming, and certainly life itself.

But not the Epiphany light. It should guide us into Lent. I remember a print of Holman Hunt's *The Light of the World*, which hung in my bedroom when I was a boy. I feared it more than I liked it: the carrier of the lantern so tall and strange, the two crowns, one of shining gold, the other of thorns. But, later, I discovered that it was painted in an English garden – one not unlike mine, a bit prickly, needing some keeping in order, and in which robins and blackbirds sang at all times of the year. Although not now, not in a hard frost, not in a landscape that is momentarily soundless.

FEBRUARY

Prisoners' Lessons

THIS year's first day's gardening. Mostly mulchy raking. Robins for company, of course. Clouds like serial duvets overhead. A wintry serenity, and everything still. In the village, 'We'll pay for this.' What with? Being a devotee of the 'now', I pass on.

I clear the gravel moat that I dug round the old house ages ago to dry it out once and for all. What a success! It is snug down under. I am reminded of my friend John Nash's delight in painting inside gravel pits and similar abandoned workings, and of his tenderness towards rusty machinery, flywheels, cogs, boilers, corrugated iron – cast-off things which once sprang into life, and which shelter below the landscape. His was, on the whole, a pre-plastic universe.

Endless snowdrops, each one so pure, so perfect. Candlemas bells was what they used to call them. The Gloire de Dijon roses will bloom from year to year without ceasing. But a good time for mud, which is everywhere. It, too, is rich, in its way.

Haphazardly, in one of those drifts of daydreams where one thing leads to another, I find myself back in Coleridge's cottage at Nether Stowey. Having just thrown a sheet over my geraniums, I am sitting in the small room where he rocked his baby son with one hand, and wrote 'Frost at Midnight' with the other. He was writing as he would never write again.

Forever Wormingford

His youthful friend Wordsworth, up the road, was doing the same. They were making a book, *Lyrical Ballads*, which would change English poetry. Walking about at night instead of in the daytime, they caused scandal. They could not pay their bills. Who were they? Call the police! So much of our greatest literature was fashioned on the hoof. Or in the extreme opposite, prison.

St Paul might not have written his Letters if he had been allowed to preach. John Bunyan's preaching was all too dangerous; so they put him in a cell to stop it. So he wrote endlessly, *The Pilgrim's Progress*, *The Heavenly Footman*, intoxicating walk-books. They were long walks through Bedfordshire.

Alan and I once followed in Bunyan's steps, and noted where he had translated his native county into a route to God. For instance, the far-off Chilterns were the Celestial Mountains; and the mansion where Bunyan had to mend the pots and pans became the House Beautiful. We stood in its tragic wreckage, imagining its music, its talk, the paintings on its walls, its flowers, its boys and girls. Its life.

I have always found ruins perfect for putting together what no longer exists. Houghton House, ruined, speaks as it never could if it was whole.

Bunyan's prison cell was close to the river where, on the bridge at curfew, a trumpet sounded to put Bedford to sleep. For him, it would suggest 'the trumpets sounding on the other side' of the Lethe. Does anyone read Bunyan now? Whenever I ask, it is: 'Oh, we did it for A level.' Set books are necessary, but those we discover for ourselves are more important.

Forever Wormingford

Our ancestors read the Bible, the Prayer Book, and Bunyan, and little else. They lived by allegory and storytelling, by what they understood to be the literal truth. Their journey was with the Comforter in *The Pilgrim's Progress*.

Bunyan was a strong man, who had to shoulder an anvil wherever he went. His genius was to correlate the walking Jesus with his walk to work – with everyone's walk to work. Today's Christian, no doubt, accompanies him on the commuter train. A large part of the day is in getting to the workplace; so it has to be more than this.

On the Road with St Paul

IT BEING too good to be inside, I check the oil tank, walk the muddy paths, and survey the snowdrops, which are legion. They clothe the rises and the hollows in their thousands, with their matchless whiteness and their sudden appearance. One day it is sodden undergrowth, the next this purity of flowers.

The birds rustle around; the sky shines. Four young horses race around the field, their coats flying. In church, I have to make up my mind whether it is after the Epiphany, or before Lent. I preach on the showing of Christ.

Religion can be neither darkness nor light, just cloudy. And there is this fading away of the brightness as the years gather. Amos – a favourite of mine – cried: 'I may not be a theologian, but I can see that things are not what they should be!' But who was going to take notice of a noisy young fruit-farmer out in the sticks? But I love his voice. It is new and non-liturgical. And beautiful. Very clear.

Forever Wormingford

In mid-Epiphany, we have St Paul on his restless travels, church-founding, magisterial. Confident – Tarsus bred men of letters. It was on the old caravan route from Asia to Europe. Tent-making in such a city was a profitable trade. We read about him during the Epiphany because the blinding light of his conversion meets the greater light. He was on the road because his deliverer had said: 'I am the light of the world.'

On his way, Paul had met Timothy, a man of mixed race, with his Greek father and Jewish mother. So they walked on, the pair of them, teaching what the friends of Jesus had taught them.

When Paul reached Troas, he had a vision – more light. Someone in his head was begging him to 'come over into Macedonia, and help us'. Leave your native east, and come to Europe. Why not? He had a Roman passport. First, he and young Timothy made for Philippi, where Paul founded perhaps his favourite church. 'I thank my God for every remembrance of you,' he would say in his letter.

His first encounter with a Philippian was near the water's edge. Walking to it on the sabbath, he had found a women's prayer-meeting in progress. He and Timothy sat down and took part. This was St Paul's first Christian activity in Europe. One of the women was a businessperson named Lydia. Having heard Paul preach Christianity, she is the first named European to become part of the Church: this woman who sold purple cloth.

His next encounter was with a girl who had been forced into fortune-telling because of her profitable madness. Along with the gospel came the light of reason. 'Be affectionate with one another,' Paul told the infant Church.

Forever Wormingford

He foresaw the multiplicity of behaviours that must enter a universal faith – it takes all sorts to make a world – and yet 'Be kind to one another.' The Church must not be monolithic, but various. Because Lydia ran a house church, she could be described as the first Christian priest in Europe, if one might be fanciful.

On a spring-in-winter day, with the Stour bursting its banks, a formlessness takes over the familiar landscape; something uncontrollable is in power. Pretty rivers swell into terrible giants. Water, water everywhere, although no rain to speak of. My ditches roar. And all these snowdrops! And the wild duck wherring over.

The Lengthening of the Light

'MIDWINTER spring is its own season', T. S. Eliot said, aptly for this moment. Certainly there is no other time like it. The bright deceiving sun, the growth which is unlike any other growth. I savour it to acknowledge its fleeting presence.

My *Garrya* blooms lopsidedly, all tassels one side, just leaf stubs the other. But countless saffron and accusing heaps of withered leaves. So I must make a start, as they say. Making a start is harder than all the rest put together. Tremendous birdsong, hurrying ditches, patches of warmth. And Ash Wednesday just over the hill.

I look back on glimmerings of mortality when I knelt before the priest and he before me as we drew crosses on our foreheads in the sanctuary. Lent, the lengthening of the light, may have begun with the fast which preceded baptism. They say that it was very strict. Barely a bite before Vespers. Fish gradually crept in. Purple vestments and no Alleluyas. All

Forever Wormingford

this grew unobserved until John Henry Newman. I recall my surprise at seeing sackcloth hiding the glories of the sanctuary at Southwark Cathedral, and my strengthening of faith as a black woman knelt before it in what seemed to be a great silence. One is supposed to see only Christ but often it is the Saviour in others.

And of course I re-read the *Four Quartets*. The blitz was wrecking London when they were written. Their Cockney chat inter-leaves a New England comprehension of London in a now classic sense and, far away at Little Gidding, I am reminded that 'Midwinter spring its own season'. Which is how it is at this moment, the final days of February attempting to desist all connection with what at school we sang as 'Winter wild and winter drear, surely winter-tide is here'. 'We will pay for this – you'll see!' they used to say in the village. But no longer. Weather is more to be experienced on the screen than in the dash between car and building. As boys we walked miles in gale and snow, half-skating, fully puffing it out, our boots elevated by ice soles, our breath preceding us 'In the dark time of the year'.

At midnight, calling in the garden for the white cat, the planes fly over, tipping a little towards Stansted as seat-belts are fastened and novels are closed, and the universe itself tilts. Yet there is almost no sound and the planes are so near to each other that it is hard to see how they can drop like vast flakes onto the Essex countryside.

My aspens shiver and my neighbour's horses have an impromptu Derby in the night air, galloping from hedge to hedge. The only thing these creatures do in their entire lifetime is to give a girl a ride on a Sunday morning. Otherwise they converse, stand stock-still, and of course think. They

Forever Wormingford

stand beneath oaks which the farmer planted when his men were at Gallipoli or ran off to be slaughtered by Wellington.

My telephone-line threads through them. The returning birds will soon be resting on them, their mouths stuffed with this year's home. Once it begins, March is a race. My hyacinths are polished stubs and last year's litter must be combed out of this year's buds. Lent must be released from the prayer book once more and its severity felt, if only gently, 'seeing that we have no power to help ourselves'.

Midwinter Spring

THE farm track lurches along from puddle to puddle. The unseen brook below me is a village Tiber. The air is soft, the sky low and colourless. But the catkins – never such pollen ropes! They swing like censers, rocking the blackbirds. We are to remember the apostle Matthias and George Herbert: the first by the luck of the draw, the second by his poetry. And still they promise rain. But the rain is a treat, being so soft and languid. Now and then, a little wind troubles the bare trees.

We await a priest and some shuffling of the benefice. Each vicar is a little reign. We say: 'In Arthur's time . . .' or 'In John's time . . .' So far, not in a woman's time, although we would be glad to say this. Our only stipulation is that an incumbent should enjoy what is here, the tremendous view of the Stour Valley, the unstoppable flood by the church gates as an ancient waterway breaks cover.

Water is an imperious element that insists on its own ways, and this is all part of the most celebrated river in English art. John Constable splashed his way through miles of it. And I

Forever Wormingford

remember the water-meadows further upstream, how they turned into seas in late winter, with gulls flocking over them and ditchers busy in them. Sodden toil. Wet feet – no wellingtons, army greatcoats, and a sense of uselessness as the floods did whatever they liked, year after year.

Below the village, old cuts and solutions are evidence of attempts to manage the flow. But nothing like the Somerset Levels, where the inhabitants blame the authorities, knowing in their hearts that nothing can be done.

It is the time to stare at flint towers. Bar a few granite boulders dragged in our direction during the Ice Age, all we have is flint, and this in abundance. It became our jewellery. Rich men wrote their names in it on the churches they created. It was a mineral blackletter which did not weather, but which stayed sharp and glassy. And never so polished as in a wet Lent.

Tramping around my old Suffolk village the other day, there on the foot of the tower, was the indelible flint homage to the Virgin Mary, bright as a button. Some unknown stone artist made it – set it – centuries before the Reformation. Neither man nor winter could rub it out.

Adrian will soon tidy up the garden for the spring. It will take its shape once more. At the moment, it is all hellebores – 'showy flowers and poisonous parts', the dictionary says, primly. And fine they are. Best not to walk anywhere other than on a solid path. The underlying squelch speaks of a garden floating on lakes.

And Ash Wednesday looms. Like a good Christian, I read T. S. Eliot: 'Midwinter spring is its own season'.

MARCH

Stony Ground

MID-LENT. Stony imagery that contrasts with the spring. The Essene boys – the pious ones – make their way to the desert. 'Now don't overdo it,' their mothers say. Jesus is old for this kind of test. Nor will it end when he returns from the wilderness both of landscape and decision.

George Herbert, who is about his age, steps into a wrecked church. More wild behaviour. Paul reminds the Thessalonians that he has taught them 'how to walk'. Their difficulty could be that they live in a lovely plain, not on stony ground.

My Stour-side land is not conducive to harsh religious behaviour at this moment, being flooded with flowers and much visited by birds, and softened by low skies. I read of Christ's illness from that extreme self-testing in the Palestinian wastes with wonderment, as should we all.

Richard Mabey comes to lunch. I suppose we could count each other as the oldest of our friends. We have lamb's liver, onions, potatoes, baked parsnips, and a glass of champagne because it is his birthday. And sit by blazing willow logs, each having finished our latest books: his about Flora Thompson, mine about Benjamin Britten. The white cat sleeps on us in turn.

We talk about Roger Deacon, a marvellous writer who had been given a perpetual young man's view of the countryside, and who swam wherever there was water: in the sea, in his pond, in the river. He was somehow mature, although he had never quite grown up – a great achievement.

In church, I talk of St John of the Cross, someone I save up for Lent. If the South African poet Roy Campbell had not managed to save his papers during the carnage of the Spanish Civil War, this St John might have become nothing more than yet another vague person on the calendar. Instead, he is startlingly vivid on account of his Christ's being the bridegroom of the Gospels.

When a woman told St John of the Cross that her prayer consisted of 'Considering the beauty of God and rejoicing that he had such beauty', he found the imagery he needed for his poetry. It was that of the seeking lover – the seeking lover on both sides. The scenes in which the Lord and his friend search for one another are in the wild landscape of Toledo. These craggy solitudes are filled with their love and desire for each other.

Cathedrals can be Toledos when the services die away, and especially when the doors close and the sightseers' footsteps fade away, and the arches speak their stony language. It is then that they might have something non-architectural to say.

St John of the Cross was not popular. He worked too hard. He was also, they complained, a crony of St Teresa of Avila. And he was, as some poets are, very accusatory at times. Like the desert. So they put him in prison to shut him up. But whether in prison, or in his cell, or by his favourite spot, the River Guadalimar, the blessed solitude was there, and he heard:

The music without sound,
The solitude that clamours,
The supper that revives us and enamours.

Forever Wormingford
Window Songs

LONG ago, I would take over a remote Suffolk church and read George Herbert to a hustled-up congregation: myself, and three writers who lived in and around Colchester. They were my guru James Turner; the South African poet R. N. Currey; and the Ulster poet W. R. Rodgers. There we would be, our breath clouding the cold nave, turning each ancient spot into another Bemerton.

Currey's family were distinguished Methodists; 'Berty' Rodgers had been a minister; and I was yet to be anything, with everything to play for. Or to live for. I was, of course, writing – but secretly, my friends being older and established. I was pretty good at programming, and at being enthusiastic where Herbert was concerned.

And there would be my first visit to Salisbury; and, many years later, a kind of implanting of part of my life there. I entered Herbert's little church for the first time, holding on to the iron latch that he himself touched four times a day, and eventually giving his silver cup to those who were kneeling where he had knelt. It had been kept in a glass case in Salisbury Cathedral, but soon Canon Judy Rees would take it back to where it belonged.

And my friend Vikram Seth would buy Herbert's rectory, where, unbeknown to anybody, Herbert would write the greatest poetry in the Anglican language. And where he died in the room next to mine, one February day, choking with the fenny ague. Yet singing!

Vikram and I once strolled in the darkening Stour marshes, as I identified for him reeds and flowers. Herbert was a tall, thin, ailing man, who rode, not walked. 'This is where he kept

Forever Wormingford

his horse,' Vikram said, pointing to a small meadow. And we sat by his hearth, the logs spitting and blazing.

He sang his window-songs morning and evening, to the lute. To go to heaven at 39 would not have been an early death, then. His mother, Magdalen Herbert, a great lady, would sometimes lay a place for Jesus at her dinner-table. But Herbert would run into him at the 'ordinary' in some inn. The ordinary was the main meal in a pub, where you sat down with everyone who happened to be there, and where there was no being above or below the salt.

It was the tradition for great folk to come to church at sermon-time only, but when his aristocratic family did this at Bemerton, Herbert locked them out. He wrote a rather severe guide to country worship, and to rural priesthood itself. Much of it still stands up.

My Herbert rule-book is his exposition on church architecture. Pevsner would have bewildered him. Being who he was, he could have had a Cambridge college, or some semi-wrecked cathedral, but all he asked for was a ruined village altar. It would last him less than two years.

Herbert was born, wed, and carried to his grave in February, too concerned with heaven to stand another English spring. The seventeenth century was nipped to the bone by ice and snow. The Thames – and the Wiltshire Stour – were frozen over for months at a time. I imagine him sitting by Vikram's fire, rubbing his dying hands, and calling for ink and paper.

The house was full of anxious women: wife, nieces, maids. But he was far away, thinking of Little Gidding, and that fat parcel of poems that had to reach there before another spring.

Forever Wormingford
A Writer Must Always Have Something to Say

WE VERGE on Lent 3. David and I bump along the valley floor in his Land Rover. Ploughs are out everywhere; the gulls are spoilt for choice. Owing to the rain, nothing could be done until today. The sodden months passed one by one, and then – this perfect growing week for the loam-marsh farmers. Their immense machines rock and roll on either side, and have the companionship of birds. We ride through the distant view in Gainsborough's *Cornard Wood*, and between the birthplaces of two hymns: 'Hills of the North, rejoice!' and 'My song is love unknown'.

My friend Margaret from Scotland is the priest for this holy landscape, and her husband is the Reader. I know it like the back of my hand, and have to be careful not to bore David with this knowledge. So I listen to his farm-talk with gratitude, keeping an eye on the ploughing, and the gull snowstorm that almost blinds the tractors, and feeling the March gladness when we enter the twisting ravine that announces Sudbury.

To the left, although I keep him to myself, is James Samson, a medieval priest in full rig, a brass fashion-plate for those who like to dress up, and who died in 1349. The Stour writhes and glitters through these old inhabitants. Its muddy fields are drying out. Its seeds are taking. Its temperature is rising. Its air is delicious.

Back at the ranch, we step into floods of snowdrops. The white cat mutters at blackbirds through the window. I find something to say for Sunday. A writer must always have something to say, else all is lost. I water the pot-plants, and

Forever Wormingford

promise them freedom once the May frosts have gone. Not long now. Ash logs are piled to comforting heights in the brick corner. I rake off its winter carpet of moss from the cat-slide roof whose tiles at this point are only five feet from the ground – not that the white cat has ever slid down it, being decorous and contemplative by nature, and not scatty. Also bone idle. Although this is a slur, for who knows what a cat is thinking? Who knows what is sleep, and what is contemplation?

All that is certain at this moment is that the spring has come and that the crops know it. And that the Ash Wednesday collect must be said after each Lenten collect.

A book of harsh black-and-white photographs arrives from Germany. The peasant flesh is ploughed with weather and toil; the farm buildings are tottering, but will never fall. The photographer Wolf-Dietmar Unterwegers has an eye for wear and tear. For snowy hair and bitter weather. For the decay of buildings and bodies. For the beauty of what is vanishing. There were Suffolk farms and Suffolk workers who looked like this when I was a boy. Tousled old men, enduring old women, tottering barns, bleached iron, still 'useful' bits and pieces. And the cold! When was I last cold, like the people in this shivery book? And their clothes so thin. And their hands so prayerful. I shall make it my Lenten study.

But then there is the Benedicite to be sung. And that is another story. 'You will find it at the back of the green prayer-book,' I tell the congregation. And the Franciscan repetitions fill the ancient church. The choir keeps its coats on and doesn't robe. The Pope flies away in a helicopter. The past is fast asleep; the birds are wide awake.

Forever Wormingford
At Blythburgh

EVERY dawn, I observe the day as it frames itself in the east window. No radio or telly, not a sound. Just the tap of the climbers on the wall. The sky is scrambled mushroom and gold. Silent birds tour the hill. This morning, Blythburgh Church enters my head. Botticelli was painting *The Magnificat* and Malory was writing *Le Morte d'Arthur* when it was being built. But who designed it? No one is likely to know. It is almost impossibly beautiful as it stands above the estuary.

Lent would have been its heyday, financially speaking; for it thrived on the revenues from fish for fasts – herrings, mostly. When these were taken away, it could do nothing but bleach in the Suffolk air. Unusually, a stone Trinity stares out to sea from the east gable: Son on Father's lap, Paraclete on Father's head.

Once, on one of my impetuous pilgrimages, I found a coffined lad, all by himself before the altar. He lay like an offering on the undertaker's trestles. I read his name on the plate, but have forgotten it. He should have been sailing. I thought how Jesus had brought only the young back to life, never the old. Or as far as we have been told.

Near the coffin, the sons of the Dutch marsh-drainers had carved their names on the stalls and chopped out holes for inkwells. 'Dirck Lowerson von Stockholm Anno 1665.' Everywhere else, it is M for the Virgin in flint.

This is reluctant archbishops' week. Not only Rowan, but Cuthbert and Cranmer. Saxon saints in particular were in flight from bishoprics. The least glimpse of holiness and one was enthroned. Oh, for the cave by the sounding shore! This is also the week when they murdered Archbishop Oscar

Forever Wormingford

Romero at his altar. How I detest those who, knowing so little about the faith, say that this or that bishop 'should give a lead'. Meaning that they should pronounce on every religious thing. 'Who doth ambition shun?' – surprisingly, many a name on the Calendar.

Wild garlic grows on the stream bank, and bluebells on the track bank, both in profusion. How long they have been doing this, heaven alone knows. And there is no sign of drought, other than on the fields. Mercifully, they might not cull my badgers but inoculate them. No good would have come from culling, anyway; also, cows are few and far between in the valley – Tom's enchanting Lincolns, red in the new grass, excepted. Badger or any other slaughter is a Herod remedy. It never works.

David has found a baby muntjac in his orchard, bellowing away. These are Javanese escapees from the Duke of Bedford's park, I am told. Now and then, they crash about in my wood, then move on like a lost tribe looking for its rightful home. They say they taste good.

In Blythburgh Church, there is a fifteenth-century carving of pig-killing. Also of angels with springing curls and wings, and semi-smiles. They fly in the marine air. Is their message delivered? Do they know who made them? I can see the late-medieval carpenter licking his pencil and sharpening his adze, calling for paint and a ladder. IHS he scrawls everywhere.

The Unsheltered

RAW spring days. The wind whistles through the thin hedge. There is a profusion of birds and primroses. Duncan's fields

Forever Wormingford

have been polished by cold rains. I rake up ancient leaves, for the oilman cometh. The small tanker, bringing a year's warmth, will float to me on a bed of leaves, and the driver and I will fervently pray for a safe delivery, for the tractor not to be called on. He has a glass of milk. He has been a soldier, and has a way with enormous vehicles. I am safe until next April.

Writing is a static activity. Artists move about, shifting this way and that. My friend John Nash stood with his back to the north light from ten until four every day, regular as clockwork. Sandwiches arrived at one sharp; tea was by the fire, or in the garden. When he and his wife went to Cornwall or Scotland twice a year, he cleared a place in the studio for me to write. But I wrote outside in the garden when it was hot, and downstairs by the Rayburn when it was cold.

The great rural poet John Clare often wrote in hiding, lying low in a field or under a hedge, so that the neighbours could not see a ploughman engaged in matters which were none of his business. But he compared himself to the nightingale who 'hides and sings'. He led a double life in the village, although eventually it became a marvellous single existence of traditional labour, and the right words to describe it. Those who had previously written about the land and its seasonal demands had rarely put a hand to it; after Clare, it would be different.

Much of my writing is done on a rickety kitchen table under a fruit tree, although indoors I write with my back to the window, as the view is distracting. Somehow, this is no view when I am in it. And especially when digging and raking, keeping my eyes on the ground. Now I must make the sweet-pea wigwam.

Forever Wormingford

My friend Tony Venison is due. Learned and appreciative, for many years his gardening column in *Country Life* guided us all. We met in the garden which Sir Cedric Morris created at Hadleigh, a few miles away, and Tony has inherited both its workaday genius and its spell. We will sit in the pub and go over our past.

Mutuality is a marvellous thing, especially when it is controlled by a shared learning – although here I have to confess that mine has stopped somewhere at the elementary stage where gardening is concerned. But I am an expert and tireless, or uncomplaining, weeder. According to religion, Paradise, a sheltered garden, is where we should be. My first botany was in one of those Bibles which did not end with Revelation, but with a list of plants. And I sometimes hear God questioning us as we enter Paradise: 'My beautiful Earth; why didn't you enjoy it more, its trees and flowers?'

Lent is a kind of fertilization of the spirit. It is the time when we have to find the space to let it grow. Its desert must bloom. I find that simplicity, not self-denial, is the better aid for this. It is what the Quakers tell us. I have just given a talk in their meeting house in Sudbury, Suffolk, my home town, and felt quietly blessed all the time.

Alice in Oxford

OXFORD in the rain. The cobbles shine; the colleges have emptied. But the city is full for the Literary Festival. From my window at Christ Church, I am able to look into Alice's garden. Japanese tourists pass by in scores and dozens, each group holding up a banner that says 'Excelsior' in Japanese, and pointing scores and dozens of cameras. Plastic-wrapped because of the rain, they seem indefatigable in their sightseeing.

Peering through my window, what would Lewis Carroll have made of them? *Alice in Wonderland* ends with an Easter greeting to 'every child who loves *Alice*'.

But it is Passiontide, and resurrection is far off. Joggers, young and old, pass by, some with puzzled dogs, all soaked to the skin. But the rain is soft and without bitterness. They run to the river, some with wide leaps, others with little tottering steps. The Japanese pass with flocking movements, like gentle chickens, and sometimes hand in hand.

I walk to the Bodleian Library where, surprisingly, tea has been laid on a vast table. But no Mad Hatter, just Henrietta Garnett and myself to manage hefty scones and our audience. We are to talk about our houses, Charleston and Bottengoms. Each of them smells – of turpentine, paraffin oil from a previous occupancy, our old friends, artists, and the like. And so the visit passes.

Oxford becomes more and more beautiful beneath its spring scrubbing. Sad music flows from its tiny cathedral, and I halt to listen. At the endless tea-party, I am joined by Mr Binyon, whose Great-Uncle Laurence wrote *For the Fallen*, and by Diarmaid MacCulloch, who has just written *Silence: A Christian History*. Only, no one holds their tongue; for it is a literature festival, when writers chatter. And the constant rain does the reverse of putting a damper on our proceedings. Its stimulation is felt inside and out.

Back at Christ Church, going to bed, I am horrified to discover that there is nothing to read, other than the book I have written myself, and what good is that? Not a single volume exists in the tall rooms, not so much as a newspaper lining in

Forever Wormingford

the drawers, only a card telling the time of breakfast. Lucky Alice had found a book called *Jabberwocky* – maybe in this very room, fortunate girl. But all I could do was put the light out and starve for print. Outside, in the dark, her trees were greedily drinking the March rain.

Lewis Carroll finished writing *Through the Looking Glass* just before Easter 1876, ending it with another Easter greeting. 'Do you know that delicious dreamy feeling,' he says, 'when, lying lazily, with eyes half-shut, one sees as in a dream green boughs waving and waters rippling in a golden light? It is a pleasure very near to sadness . . .'

Will the Japanese boys and girls in their hotels be developing their understanding of Oxford from a thousand photos? Will the joggers be setting forth to nowhere? Will the white cat – named after Alice's cat, Kitty – be despairing?

Still pouring, the car leaves the lovely wet city for home. The festival folk have given me a hamper. It includes a book – Max Beerbohm's *Zuleika Dobson*, which I read when I was a teenager – and lots of biscuits and sandwiches. And so the day closed.

Teachers

THIS delectable springtime continues. Lunch in the garden on Sunday after matins. All the birds operatic. The horses on the sloping meadows benign. The Wordsworthian daffodils under the budding fruit trees making a show. 'They make a show,' an elderly woman said as she planted asters. But no show in church. Lent is plain fare.

I must remember to see the hares' boxing-match over my horizon. Sparring would be a better word to describe their activity. Meanwhile my badgers hump and trundle themselves through the orchard to the cold-running stream, leaving a highway through the shooting grass. As for daffodils, they have lost all sense of proportion, and wave everywhere, trumpeting their worth to the skies.

At the poetry society, Andrew and I pay homage to Mrs Girling, a Georgian lady who founded our school 100 years before the 1870 Education Act. Where would we have been without her? I think of John Clare being taught to read and write in the vestry, and of boys such as Thomas Bewick who were encouraged to draw on the smooth surfaces of the stone floor in church. Or, much earlier, the women who taught themselves to read from chained Bibles. I got the hang of the Holy Land as I pored over the maps at the back of Revelation during Canon Hughes's sermons.

William Hazlitt wrote tenderly about such things as he saw his old father, a man who had suffered greatly for his radical stance, 'withdrawn from the world of all of us'.

He goes on:

After being tossed about from congregation to congregation [he was an Irish Unitarian minister] . . . he had been relegated to an obscure village, where he was to spend the last thirty years of his life, far from the only converse that he loved, the talk about disputed texts of Scripture, and the causes of civil and religious liberty.

> Here he passed his days . . . in the study of the Bible, and the perusal of the Commentators – huge folios, not easily got through, one of which would outlast a winter! . . . glimmering notions of the patriarchal wanderings, with palm trees hovering in the horizon, and processions of

camels at the distance of three thousand years . . . questions as to the date of creation, predictions of the end of all things; the great lapses of time, the strange mutations of the globe were unfolded with the voluminous leaf, as it turned over . . .

My father's life was comparatively a dream; but it was a dream of infinity and eternity, of death, the resurrection, and a judgement to come.

I have always loved this passage by Hazlitt, a young man who no longer believed what his father believed. The most honest and in its way shocking example of this dilemma is, of course, Edmund Gosse's *Father and Son.* One needs to be brave to read it.

Turning to the altar, I say 'I believe', thankful for the formula but never analysing it. *Credo.* Somewhat lost in it, like old Mr Hazlitt's camels, is my love of Christ as it journeys on from year to year, expanding, narrowing, leading ahead. Liturgy takes me over deserts. And then there is George Herbert's 'dear prayer', with or without words.

'Let us pray,' I say to the familiar faces which look towards me, and they gently acquiesce. The other Sunday I said Robert Louis Stevenson's prayers – the ones he said in Samoa – and they suited us very well, talking as they did to God and his 'household'.

APRIL

Mrs Fox's Fritillary Field

AS ALWAYS, the fritillaries halt me in my tracks. Since I search eagerly for most seasonal treasures, I have never understood why a small group of them under the walnut tree are not seen until they wave at me to stop. They are about a foot high, and stand up well in the not-quite-mature spring grass. Each bloom has six matt, lustreless petals, and it declines rather than droops, with dark threadlike stalks. Every April and May, from time immemorial, they show themselves in my orchard to remind me of what I have come to think of as their native land – Framsden, in Suffolk.

It is there, at the long pasture in the dell, which is covered with these speckled, bell-shaped, vaguely sinister blooms – the British species of genus Fritillaria liliaceae. It was an hour's bike-ride from my house, and a proper pilgrimage for a member of the Wild Flower Society. And Mrs Fox, tall, elderly, and generous, standing at the gate to welcome us where snake's heads grew.

For 50 weeks her long meadow was no more than two acres of dank grass, with a lush drainage ditch severing it; but when the fritillaries came, it turned into the Plains of Enna when Persephone set foot in them. There they were – hundreds, thousands of them, some a papery white, but most a muted purple colour with the reptilian markings that gave them their nickname. Nightingales sang over them. There

Forever Wormingford

was a cold wind blowing, as well as these mysterious spring flowers.

It would have been a Saturday afternoon when Mrs Fox was at home. There were so many of them that we never knew where to tread, and when we left she would give us little fritillary bouquets. This was the time when country people believed that the more you picked the more they grew – a policy that rioted when it came to bluebells.

Fritillaries were so called by the Romans after their dice-box, or shaker, which was one of the few personal belongings that a soldier carried around. This, and a chequer-board. 'And they crucified him, and parted his garments, casting lots, that it might be fulfilled which was spoken by the prophet, They parted my garments among them and upon my vesture did they cast lots.'

Matthias succeeded the tragic Judas by the luck of the draw. The rattling dice-boxes decided great matters. And here is this dicey flower, with its suggestive markings, among the primroses every year in my garden – often a meal for blackbirds if I don't protect it.

I will keep those that Mrs Fox gave me until they shrivel to nothing on my desk, but I never pick mine. I walk to them, and watch them. And tread around them. Tidying up a 'Rambling Rector' rose so that it knows its place; hanging up a fallen apple branch; raking sodden leaves; and hearing the rooks carrying on, thinking of Framsden and Mrs Fox and her countless snake's heads. – 'Put them in water as soon as you get home, dear. They'll last: you'll see!' And her joyous dog – 'Get you down!'

I must make a proper remembrance of Framsden, and place a single snake's head on the windowsill, but the wind, how icy it is, and the nesting birds, how they sing! And the continuity of all things. At matins, we sing the Benedicite: 'O all ye fritillaries, bless ye the Lord. Praise him and magnify him for ever.'

The Lady Julian

I AM apt to forget that old neighbours are likely to know the interior of my old house as well as I do. The garden and wood, too, of course. The other day, David told me about my black-leaved blackberries. And I showed him the walnut tree that had been planted for his parents' golden wedding.

The babysitters of the inter-war years are few on the ground; ditto the old chaps in the snapshots who tiffled about with hoes and scythes. And the lads drinking Tizer on the wall are likely to be no more. But the pond plants are golden every spring. They found blackberry seeds in the tummy of the Neolithic man who was taken from his grave at Walton-on-the-Naze, I was told.

A long time ago, a very ancient person came to see me, wondering if he could still hear the church clock strike from the pear tree. He could.

'Hev you still got that ol' glasshouse?'

'It collapsed.'

'I'm grieved to hear that.'

It is Passiontide, and I am thinking of the Lady Julian. Not that it is her time, but she comes into my head now and then. I am thinking of her account of the crucifixion, which I hardly dare read, though I must. We all should.

And the words of Christ dying came to mind. 'I thirst.' I saw that he was thirsty in a twofold sense, physical and spiritual . . . That his blessed frame was drained of all blood and moisture . . . What could be seen of the skin of the face was covered with tiny wrinkles, and was tan-coloured; it was like a plank when it has been planed and dried out. The face was browner than the body . . . He was hanging in the air like some cloth hung out to dry.

Julian the writer is the mistress of aridity. Hers is the dustiest language we have for the desert experience. But, when she describes Newman's 'second Adam' in gardening imagery, she really does make the rain fall and the streams flow. God is the master, his Son the servant.

The latter is 'dressed simply, like a man ready for work – "He was wearing a single white coat, old and worn." For he was to be a gardener, digging and banking, toiling and sweating, turning and trenching the ground, watering the plants the while. And by keeping at this work he would make sweet streams to flow, fine abundant fruits to grow; he would bring them to his lord, and serve them to his taste.'

From her window on the world, Julian would have seen the River Wensum in flood, and the orchards of her Norwich neighbours. Also a scaffold, maybe. They say that Celtic crosses do not show the crucified Jesus, but the risen Lord. We sang 'My song is love unknown' at evensong. It is a play on George Herbert's poem 'Love Unknown', and it, too, rehearses the appalling nature of the crucifixion, although not with Julian's realism.

The media never draw the line. Young bodies show their mutilations while we eat and chat. The Cross dangles from bracelets. I preach on contemplation, knowing that neither I nor my listeners are able to see what Julian saw.

Forever Wormingford

Digging

HOLY WEEK. A soft gale troubles the bare trees. But it will not rain. Gulls land among the horses. The stream pours unseen to the river. The garden calls.

I re-read Julian's revelations of divine love in which, for me, there is an unparalleled account of the crucifixion – one that could only have been written by someone who had witnessed official torture. Also a slow dying. It comes after Julian's enchanting comparison of God's love to a hazelnut. 'What is this? It is all that is made.'

She translates medieval Christianity in a way that makes it acceptable to us, all these centuries later, and never more so than when she describes what happened on Good Friday. Without writers like her, 'We do not know, we cannot tell, what pains he had to bear.'

And yet her Christ is a gardener sent by his master to plant love in his creation, digging and banking, toiling and sweating, turning and trenching the ground, watering the plants the while.

'And by keeping at this work he would make sweet streams to flow, fine abundant fruit to grow; he would bring them to his lord, and serve them to his taste.'

Although a young neighbour does most of the sweating and turning these days for me, I can look on the Bottengoms garden with some pride at the hard graft that created it, long ago.

In fact, I love digging, especially in the kitchen garden, where the soil fell off the spade in delectable clumps, and robins followed me up and down, up and down, and the mower made its neat mark; and the excitement of deciding where the runner beans should climb this summer could be intoxicating. So when a friend came to tell me about his London allotment, my heart went out to him.

And when I visited the Garden Museum in Lambeth, its relics spoke more of human happiness than mere toiling and sweating.

Anyway, I have made a start. The white cat looks down at me from a tree. Nesting birds watch anxiously from ivy grandstands. Bluebells, their buds still near to their roots, perilously close to the badger setts, promise a show in May; and, altogether, I have made a start. Making a start is the thing. One cannot do it often enough.

How terrible it was that Jesus had to suffer in a garden – probably one that he knew and delighted in; one in which ancient olives were rooted in Jewish history: Gethsemane.

He had walked there after the Last Supper, accompanied by his disciples. He would have crossed the brook, Kidron, and descended the little valley between Jerusalem and the Mount of Olives.

It was springtime, and Julian of Norwich walked with Christ in Gethsemane. She was a young woman of 30, and was not well, but 'thought it a pity to die'. And rose from her bed because she had much to say.

It was 8 May 1373. It was then that she wrote her masterpiece. It became illegible with time, as we all do; but a modern scholar, Clifton Walters, brushed the grave-dirt from it so that we could find our way about in Holy Week, meeting the gardener and saviour, and be forced to comprehend his crucifixion, and attempts to uproot him, and then to arrive at his glorious flowering.

Forever Wormingford
Cleaning Winter off the Windows

IN THE old liturgy, there are readings for Monday and Tuesday in Easter Week, then a great jump to the First Sunday, the content of these readings being more than enough for any Christian to contemplate. Their stories are filled with physicality, of eating and walking. The resurrected Jesus walks all the way to Emmaus – seven miles – and turns supper into the eucharist; says, 'Handle me: I'm not some ghost.'

The spring weather has to be imagined, but one senses its brightness. What is evident is normality, a carefulness not to give hostage to myth. There is fish and honeycomb and wine and bread. The cross is referred to as 'the tree' – as itself a living thing. In reality, it would have been used to put to death many a poor criminal. Divinely perceived, it drew to it glorious words, some of them spoken by the tree itself.

My trees shake in the cold April air. Shake and crack. Never so many birds. And thousands of flowers, all the first daffodils and the lasting hellebores. I crave warmth. A day to put a chair outside. I have been doing the proofs of a new book, re-reading each page line by line, lifting the illiterate cat from my copy, telling it a tale, making coffee for callers, cleaning winter off the windows, working hard. The snow takes its time to go away. Patches of it cling to the hillside for dear life. The sun turns a horse's whirling tail into spun glass. Acres of vegetables should be 'getting going'. I fill in a great hole in my track with broken bricks and flints, while dogs come to watch. The Little Horkesley church clock tells the hours vaguely. Kites float overhead. And, lo and behold!, the sun heats up.

Forever Wormingford

There is a proverb that says: 'A snow year, a rich year.' George Herbert collected it. Tell this to the journalists who cannot stop going crazy when it comes to weather. They are the best-dressed people on TV, have you noticed? None of their clothes have been out in the rain. And correctly so; for our weather is our religion, and its forecasters are our priests. Their smiles! Their smart vestments!

At matins and evensong, I say: 'Let us remember in our hearts all those who are ill, in pain, or are having difficult treatments…' And should I wake up in the night, I do the same. Although, as I rarely wake between 11 p.m. and 6.30 a.m., sick friends tend to be sparsely prayed for. So I must adjust my petitions.

As I rarely attend the village surgery, I was surprised when the doctor shouted 'Next!' when there was only myself in the next room. He gave me 50 paracetamols, which I haven't taken, and this two years ago. But they might come in handy. You never know with the flesh. It plays one up. 'Next!' Not that I think about it. I read poems and novels, and give bookish sermons to the same old friends, week in, week out. How good they are, how uncomplaining, how godly. How well they sing the hymns I have chosen. How well the organists, Meriel and Christopher, play them. How the bell-ringers call!

> I danced on the Sabbath
>   and I cured the lame:
> the holy people
>   said it was a shame.

It won't be long now before I plant out my cuttings and mow the grass. There will be some heat in the sun, some leaves on the trees.

Forever Wormingford
My Trees

'HOW many trees have you got?' asks the little boy. One, an enormous willow, has tipped over, and he sees it split in three. A hundred, 200, I hazard. I planted a few broad-leaved ones a lifetime before he was born. To fill the spaces left by the elms. I live in a small wood, thus, tree-music is a constant.

The wood is greening at this moment – greening and whispering. I have sent a postcard of John Constable's bark-study to Dan to tell him: 'Please come on Monday.' My trees enchant him. He has been to the David Hockney exhibition, and to Paris. The Hockney wood puzzles him, as it does me. The absence of botany, shall we say.

When Constable was a lad, and walking to see his Wormingford family – 'the Wormingford folk' – he had to pass an enticing medieval park, about five miles from here, and the baronet kindly gave him a pass which said: 'Pray permit Mr Constable to draw the trees.' This so that the game-keepers did not drive him out.

Tom Gainsborough had painted *Cornard Wood* a few miles away. They say that there are more trees hereabouts now than in their day. Paul, our tree man, has to hold an inquest on my tumble-down willow – what to do? A standing tree inhabits the sky; a fallen one lives nowhere, and dies everywhere.

In the past, Christians called the Cross 'the Tree'. Fortunatus sang:

O Tree of beauty, Tree of light,
O Tree with royal purple dight,
Elect on whose triumphal breast
Those holy limbs should find their rest!

Forever Wormingford

In the Saxon poem 'The Dream of the Rood', the writer is contemplating the crucifixion.

> The finest of trees began to talk:
> 'I remember the morning, a long time ago
> That I was felled at the edge of the forest
> And severed from my roots. Strong enemies seized me
> And fashioned me for their sport, bade me hold up their felons on high . . .
> I saw the Lord of Mankind courageously hasten to climb upon me.'

My trees certainly chatter away – best of all, the aspens in summer; sotto voce, enticingly, articulating tree happiness. I lie beneath them, book unread, seduced by their soft song, like John Clare or Thomas Traherne. So much occurred under trees in the Bible. They became markers for beginnings from Eden onwards. Scripture is a virtual forest and a simple shade, a bare wood and a glorious orchard.

Our churchyard trees were planted by a Victorian priest. Should one of them depart, we introduce another. Their dust and our dust have an arrangement that suits us both. I sit under them, waiting for the ringers to approach an end. They have to be pagan in spite of our poets, which is another kind of sacredness.

There are wayside oaks that are contemporary with Arden. And, down by the river, delicate, shivery cricket-bat plantations, which are harvested every 15 or so years. An Easter full moon looked down on them.

Forever Wormingford
East Anglian Masters

I LOVE provincial art galleries. It is amazing what hangs on their walls. Is that a real Picasso? And who is this painter no one has ever heard of? It is so captivating.

This week, I went to the Minories Art Gallery, in Colchester, to see the permanent collection, which I knew existed, but had forgotten. And there they were – the artist friends of my youth, and of the Suffolk–Essex countryside I had known. Also, the ghostly assemblies I joined in a stately townhouse just after the war. I usually went with John and Christine Nash, who themselves belong to another day: John, who never looked at the paintings, and chatted away to old friends; and Christine, who sat in a tall window, endlessly embroidering.

I took in the exhibition appreciatively, longing to paint, not at all longing to write. It had been the generous custom of each artist to give a work to the gallery, and these, from having been tucked away so long, were now a kind of autobiography. Each picture, even if it was a portrait, brought to life another face, another room, another time.

There was Sir Cedric Morris, tall, his scarf tucked through a silver ring. There was my friend John Bensusan-Butt, cousin to the Pissarros. There were the poets James Turner, W. R. Rodgers, and R. M. Currie – all a generation older than myself, but we did not constitute an East Anglian collective: we were just local people who spread our wings after the war.

And, most importantly for me, there was the emergent Aldeburgh Festival, and its founders, Benjamin Britten, Imogen Holst, and Peter Pears. What there was not was

Forever Wormingford

wages, just little handouts and big improvisations. Simplicity was the thing. I walked and biked everywhere. I edited the wonderful programme books – collectors' items now – and did everything from setting out the stacked chairs to persuading the Suffolk priests to allow concerts to take place in their beautiful churches.

One of them forbade applause, and I still dislike the often excessive clapping of some concerts. There should be a few seconds at least, after the last notes of Schubert or Bach, to translate the audience to another sphere, but not this battle of palms and feet.

Everything took place in Aldeburgh itself in those days. But the spread of music across the marshes to Snape altered everything for the better. The entrepreneur Newson Garrett had built a vast maltings there in the nineteenth century, as well as emancipating women – Elizabeth Garrett Anderson was his daughter – and the entire business of concert-going was transformed by Snape.

My particular friends were Denis and Jane Garrett. He an exciting botanist, his wife a loving head of social welfare in Cambridge. Oh, brave new world! It was run on a shoestring – but a highly professional shoestring. I wrote stories, walked miles, got used to the sea, and became a writer.

At this moment, I am re-reading that Essex masterpiece, J. A. Baker's *The Peregrine*. Once read, constantly read. One could call Baker a mid-twentieth-century John Clare. There is nothing like this bird book in the whole of English natural history. Its ravishing prose and scientific force remain mysterious. It was written by a rather ill young man as he cycled in the rivery countryside around Chelmsford. Each evening, he would translate his birdwatching jottings into brilliant prose. He died in 1986, having carried birdwatching into English literature.

Jane Austen in Church

AS THE countryside swarms up, and as folly in its many disguises preoccupies the nation, let us re-read Jane Austen. And particularly *Emma*. Emma Woodhouse, you will recall, was 'handsome, clever, and rich, with a comfortable home and happy disposition', and 'seemed to unite some of the best blessings of existence, and had lived nearly 21 years in the world with very little to distress or vex her'.

Thus, both ignorant and innocent, she believes that she is qualified to run the parish. Of course, one does not have to be a rich girl to possess this ruling confidence: elderly or merely grown-up politicians with a great deal of money do the same. But it is the confidence of folly which brings unease.

This being the *Church Times*, we must first glance at Emma's religion. It should not take long. It is, of course, Austen's religion – and she the daughter of a parson! But what she knew and recorded, wrote someone who knew her, 'was the opinions and practice then prevalent among respectable and conscientious clergymen before their minds had been stirred – first by the Evangelical, and afterwards by the High Church movements'.

Thus the Church is scarcely mentioned in *Emma*, in spite of the fact that four of its main characters – Mrs and Miss Bates, and the Revd Philip Elton and Mrs Elton – could not be more closely connected with it.

Mr Elton does not suggest priestliness, and does not mention his Lord once. And Emma herself only goes to church

Forever Wormingford

twice in a long novel, and that to weddings. The ethical and social aspects of Christianity jostle every chapter, though never the spiritual. In Austen-land, however, these are the religious contours. When popular Evangelical sounds broke into her sedate Anglicanism, she said that 'they who are so far from Reason and Feeling, must be happiest'.

Death is avoided, for the most part. Its absence is comic rather than sad. 'What a blessing it is when undue influence does not survive the grave!' But money is a far more serious matter. There is a hard fiscal core to all the novels, and particularly to *Emma*. When rich Frank Churchill marries penniless Jane Fairfax, 'it wasn't a connection to gratify' – although, because of the Married Women's Property Act being far off, even if Jane had been as rich as Emma, Frank would have taken everything she possessed at the chancel step.

Sir Walter Scott, the international novelist of Austen's day, and himself writing his way out of bankruptcy, when he reviewed *Emma*, blamed the author for her mercenary view of marriage. To this she replied that if it was wrong to marry for money, it was certainly foolish to marry without it.

And so the glorious author goes her way in the twenty-first century, undated, witty, and still financially sound in our unequal world, shaking our certainties, and laughing at our pretensions. And yet mysteriously, like the old Jews, not liking to say his name even when practising his love.

She certainly knew that there was such a thing as society. It was this knowledge on which the morality of her wonderful novels depended. We use them like a measure for our own time, for what is true taste and for what is folly. Inequalities that we thought we had grown out of have returned. The immensely rich rule. There is a North and South. A funeral costs £10 million.

MAY

Cuckoo

THE first cuckoo. Its call-note is unmistakeable, the books tell me. As is its parasitic habit. Why build a nest when others can build it for you? It glides in from foreign parts to its seasonal home in the Stour Valley. It likes the edges of things, where the woods and commons peter out. Its cry is relentlessly the same for weeks on end. It stays summery and welcome, and we tell each other, 'I heard the first cuckoo this morning.' Not to have done so would be worrying, and the summer itself diminished.

It is a ruthless occupier of other birds' nests, heaving out eggs and chicks to make a home for its brood. How strange that other species are unable to tell the difference between their own brood and the invader.

That most enchanting and knowledgeable of bird poets, and tester of popular legend, John Clare, did not believe that cuckoos had hollow backs specially designed for this purpose. I, too, have found what might be called a comfortable ignorance of nature in many neighbours, although some of the TV documentaries are beginning to shift this.

Clare despaired at the way his neighbours would go thus far and no further in nature study, if one could call it that, perhaps finding it blasphemous to know more than their parents did about flowers and birds. They did not need to

Forever Wormingford

be told what a cuckoo in the nest was when it came to their own families.

Once, Clare heard both a nightingale and a cuckoo on the same evening. He hated natural history being put to use for human conduct; but he didn't get very far with science among his Northamptonshire friends. They had centuries of legend behind them, most of it full of repeated falsities, and his commands to look, listen, and learn were ignored. Even today, hearing my first cuckoo, there has been an effort to listen to a bird and not a human morality.

And there it sings, Colchester way, not too far off, a creature of variegated greys, monotonous, plaintive with early summer. 'Did you hear the cuckoo last evening?' I will say at the first opportunity; for this is the drill. And I will forget that it was last listened to in Africa, and that it is not the prerogative of an English late spring.

Meanwhile, I hesitate to pull advance wildflowers like weeds from my borders. Laburnum hangs in greening tassels, and only prejudice stops me from saying that my nettles are a sight.

In church I read, 'O Lord, from whom all good things do come: Grant to us thy humble servants that by thy holy inspiration we may think those things that be good, and by thy merciful guiding may perform the same.' And I preach on Julian of Norwich, who thought it a pity to die when one was 30. A Norfolk priest was there to catch her last words; for something told her to abandon this deathbed for literature. How it must have irritated those who stood around her: having to blow the candles out, dismiss the priest, and cope with genius.

Forever Wormingford

Adrian has mown the grass paths. I edge them. How smart we are. The lilacs are sumptuous. 'Lalocks,' my grandmother used to call them. She wouldn't have them in the house. 'Unlucky,' she would say. We brought her a bunch, but she hurried them outside. Should a bee wander in, it would mean a good message. Should there be lightning, she would cover the mirrors with cloths. For her, life was a run of blessings and risks.

Shepherd Sunday

A WILD wet day. Chilly, too. Gloire de Dijon roses rock against the window, and a squirrel is eating a crust with great delicacy on the lawn below. It nibbles as though it is playing the flute, holding the bread out at an angle, noting the crumbs.

It is barely light, and the hill where my neighbour, Mr Brown, came across the axehead looks drenched. He brought it in, and laid it on the kitchen table. 'There. Never been used.' Someone had dropped it on the high ground in the Bronze Age. What a loss. It had worked its way up through the flinty earth. We washed it under the tap, and it shone.

We imagined the finder retracing his steps a hundred times over the hill, weeping with disappointment. Maybe calling out to his axe in a language we will never know. 'The museum will tell us all about it.' Yet, in a strange way, in its worked-up state it was informative enough.

Shepherd Sunday. I preached on losing and finding – a favourite theme in the Gospels. Ages ago, someone I knew had lost his daughter to the Moonies, and when, after the

Forever Wormingford

greatest difficulties, he found her, the girl had to be helped to find him; for the sect had wiped her father from her memory.

The Gospels are full of finders and losers. The psalms, too. They preach precariousness. Yet, at the same time, they despise safety first. Both are filled with wanderers. With people getting off the beaten track in both the Temple and the synagogue, questioning, arguing. People longing to find home, but turning up in barren debates, prodigals from faith.

No sheep in sight on my hill this wet May morning, only a girl on a pre-breakfast love-errand to a horse, which looks up, then goes on grazing.

When I was a child, I used to wonder, in an Orwellian way, why farm animals – horses, particularly – tolerated hedges. Why didn't they jump over them and gallop off to Bedfordshire, this county for some reason having become a far freedom in my imagination?

Staying on the Welsh border with the poet Edward Storey, I would lie in bed waiting for morning tea, and watch Dafyd the young shepherd bring his sheep down in the soft greyness that is not at all like the Stour Valley greyness, but a kind of muted country all its own, and which I think I can smell when I reach Presteigne.

Certainly, it tells me that it is the climate that alone could produce writers such as Thomas Traherne and Henry Vaughan. The latter once prayed:

> Either disperse these mists, which blot and fill
> My perspective still as they pass,
> Or else remove me hence unto that hill,
> Where I shall need no glass.

Forever Wormingford

There are no sheepdogs in the Bible. Its shepherds do not drive sheep, like Dafyd, but lead them. 'Lead us, heavenly father, lead us.' In the vestry, the bishop unscrews his crook and fits it into a case.

Above my ancient farmhouse, Horkesley betrays its origins: from hurk – 'a temporary shelter for young lambs, formed of hurdles wattled with straw'. Lower Bottoms, the pastures of my house, lie below the track, dense with buttercups and sodden grass. Yet the old pasturage of the faith seems less evident in East Anglia than on the edge of Wales. It is those unhedged-about flocks!

Old Ladies

CHILLY May days. Lilacs cense the mown lawns. Blackbirds do their best. Horses stay still and converse. The church smells nice. I gaze anxiously at the ashes – will they escape the plague? The oaks are in full leaf, and the Stour Valley is wondrous to behold.

John and I go to the Thatchers for fish and chips, and to look at the immense view. We discuss the Etruscans to muzak, and the insatiable human need to be immemorially entombed. *The Churchyard Handbook* is not much help in this direction. It is generally believed that we will be remembered for 40 years after we are 'gone'. But the car park is full of comings and goings above the Iron Age bones. Fresh hedges are green walls, and Mount Bures' church spire thrusts into a low sky.

My existence straddles two dioceses: Chelmsford, and St Edmundsbury & Ipswich; but, since I can't drive, they are

Forever Wormingford

as unreachable as Rome for all practical purposes. Friends return from them with tales of wondrous singing and preaching. Long ago, I used to imagine what it must be like to live in a close where every day was a procession.

Down at the farmhouse, life is a procession of a writer and his cat. Today, the pair of us pause at the glorious sight of the vast laburnums in full bloom on the long walk. 'Look thy last on all things lovely,' Walter de la Mare said. Not that I feel the approach of Last Things – rather the reverse, but no one should miss May or its flowering shrubs.

I once carried an armful of lilac into my grandmother's cottage when I was a boy. Pandemonium. 'Take them out – take them out!' Then, 'Poor child, he doesn't know any better.' She was a Suffolk countrywoman born in the 1870s, and a lover of evensong, and her existence was rich with superstitions. When she saw television for the first time, she said: 'There is something I want to know: can they see us?'

Spring brings her near. It was less securely Christian than the winter, particularly May-time. But the bumble bee trapped in the window would give her unwanted messages. Now and then, Canon Hughes would sit with her of an afternoon, on his round of old ladies, his Welsh and her Suffolk voices winding in and out for the destined half an hour.

The Blythe graves tumble about in the village churchyard, their stones hardly legible. When I took an American cousin to see them, he was indignant at the wild scene. I explained that this was the wildflower bit of the churchyard, to do with saving the planet, or something. He was not appeased.

He stared at the humps and bumps of his relations, and I remembered a poem by Thomas Hardy, in which a London churchyard was destroyed to make way for a railway terminus.

Forever Wormingford

Thus peasant dust from centuries past made way for our relations, and theirs would hold a name briefly – 40 years, maybe – after which the faces of the dead would vanish from memory. The youthful cousin doubted this, too.

But the immortality of certain wildflower sites – bluebells, for instance – is something I cannot doubt or rationalize. The Tudor woman Joanna Sturdy, who cast two of our bells (she took on the business after her husband died), would have seen our Arger Fen bluebells, I am sure. Anyway, the May-time rite of going to see them is never neglected. There they are, in all their jazzy blueness and multitudinous splendour. Just where they were when we were ten.

The Reverend Francis Kilvert

MAY-TIME, when I like to read *Kilvert's Diary* to the congregation. It is not all that keen on readings, much preferring speakings without notes. I see the youthful Francis in his Clyro pulpit, trying not to see the girls. And I think of handsome Mr Elton eyeing Miss Woodhouse and her £30,000.

I look down on the same dear ones year after year, often seeing them in the places that they have vacated. The lasting enchantment of *Kilvert's Diary* is its lasting freshness. And particularly in May. It is dewy, and untouched by maturity. He would die suddenly at 39, never having quite grown up or grown out of his freshness. It was heaven's special gift to him. In May, he blooms like the plentiful flowers in this parish.

> Wednesday 13 May. This happy afternoon I went lilying in Hartham woods with sweet Georgie Gale . . . Today was the Bath Flower Show. But I would rather have gone

Forever Wormingford

lilying with sweet Georgie Gale in Hartham Woods than have gone to a hundred flower shows.

A lily of a day
Is fairer far in May

. . . We were talking of Father Ignatius and his monastery in the Black Mountains.

Kilvert's happiness came and went like our May's downpours and sunshine. Witnessing young men in habits hacking away at the soil as if they lived in the Middle Ages made him miserable. No enlightened Church of England, no girls. And when all around them in the Welsh hills the spring was in full tilt, and when clearly Robert Browning's God was in his heaven, well, it was perverse. Yet he was touched by their holiness. And thankful that he had a gardener. Parish duties aside, he needed all his energy for walking, and all his confessions for writing.

As president of the Kilvert Society, I haven't enough energy to attend its meetings on the Welsh border, but my heart is often there. And, anyway, what would the white cat, let alone our three parishes, do if I followed Kilvert around?

Herefordshire in May is both near to and distant from East Anglia. At the moment, ignorant as much of distance as of time, the white cat slumbers on an old chest. She has pushed aside a pot of dried poppy heads and a dozen novels to make a polished bed.

Outside, soaked horses devour soaking grass. Down below, the Stour is high. The lanes are better paddled than walked. Every now and then, the skies are turned off to allow me to

Forever Wormingford

mow a lawn; for life in a village is concessionary. No sooner do I go in at the first spat than green woodpeckers, collar-doves, pheasants, and chaffinches come out.

And so have all the bluebells at Tiger Hill – maybe a million of them. We all paid court to them, treading slippery paths, intoxicated by their strangely beautiful scent, awed by their psychedelic blueness. Are there words for it? A new Wayfaring tree has been planted in their azure realm. Our ancestors set *Viburnum lantana* on pilgrim routes just for ornament.

Human cruelty often stops Kilvert in his tracks. Mindless cruelties born of ignorance were part of the old rural year. Walking to the Bronith, he finds a dead blackbird in a gin. It is a late Easter, and the creature reminds him of the Cross.

The Great Barge

TO THE Stour, to launch the *John Constable*, a fine barge, or lighter, on a fine day, the populace watching, the sun shining, and a young man in danger as in *The Leaping Horse*. I have been listening to Pepys on the radio, of course. But the replica of what was once a common sight on our classic river is actual enough. David and I make our way to the water's edge, and there, perfect in every way, lies the new barge, bright as a button. May God bless all who take holiday trips in her – me first.

When I was a boy, by the Stour-side, the last Constable barges were scuttled, and lay a yard or two below the surface of the river, where it was hoped that they would feed pike, rot away, and be no more, the railway taking over. Mothers warned their swimming sons not to go near them for fear of being trapped, although this never happened. And I would watch their huge black outlines waver under the gentle current, and think of John Constable seeing them hard at work.

For him and his fellow Stour artist Tom Gainsborough, they were the most ordinary sight in the world. The river was industrial, busy all the way to the sea with these horse-drawn coalers which, to the astonishment of the Royal Academy, the young Constable, a local miller's son, imagined would be a suitable subject for art. No one bought.

In vain his glittering workaday visions of our river hung on its walls. The Stour itself twisted and turned through the water-meadows, doubling the distance to its estuary, but offering a smooth alternative to our bad roads, and the laden lighters would glide like slow birds from hard to hard, pulled by huge horses. When the old business was sunk, just before the Great War, we all thought that that was that. Progress had finished it off. Now, here I was, on a Bank Holiday afternoon, saying: 'I name this ship the *John Constable*', and climbing in, alongside a score of other river travellers, to sense the exquisite gentleness of a river journey, a fresh flag fluttering at the helm, and the blare of a bugle to say that we were coming.

Oh, we should have sailed all day! The throne we sat on provided such sensations! The afternoon was so Englishly perfect, the scattered folk on the slowly passing banks so civil, the rushing dogs in the grass so gratifyingly amazed by the sight of us, that I, at least, could have sailed on for hours; only there was a queue for others to have a turn.

So we came home to watch croquet being played in a walled garden, and to eat sandwiches.

Should paradise be in your mind, go to Sudbury, Suffolk, for a river trip on the *John Constable*. Barges are so blissful.

Forever Wormingford

And rivers are so good at getting about. They will take you to destinations that can only be dreamed of, and offer you smells that stimulate senses that you had forgotten you possessed.

Seated with other old parties on board my lighter, I saw myself, aged 14 or so, lying with a book in the water-meadows alongside the meadowsweet, the enormous East Anglian skies floating overhead. With maybe a bottle of Tizer. And the Boat Club shouts, and the screams of swallows in concert above me. And to think that all these years later they have let me launch a barge – our river's liner – and savour the early joy.

The Mesolithic Axe

THE long cold winter is running into a not-all-that-cosy May-time. But the blossom has missed the frosts, and the plum and greengage trees are very starry. My wildflower meadow is amazing, with everything from fritillaries to an about-to-burst campion, and over-wild tulips are filling it to the brim.

As for the birds, they are shouting their heads off. This morning, a loud cuckoo was almost overhead. And also fleeting clouds – the East Anglian sort, which pile up into racing armadas; so that hot sun and chilly shadows take turns in extremes. The ditches run icily to the Stour, and the ditch near the house is white with wild garlic.

David has cleared a blackberry forest, so the fine lilac can show itself off in the hedge. It is between Ascension and Whitsun, between the cloud of unknowing and Pentecost, when we should be able to see without the candles.

Forever Wormingford

A neighbour arrives at 8.30 a.m. to find me unshaven and in rags. 'I thought you got up early!' She has brought me a photo of Nat Jackson's Mesolithic axehead, picked up by the Mere the other day. On the radio, the Chief Rabbi tells us that it is 33 generations since Moses. The axe lay between shooting weeds. As always, I think of the hands that shaped it, on the high ground of the forgotten village. Somewhere under the sun.

The Mesolithics lived between Palaeolithic and the Neolithic, from 12,000 to 3000 BC, and in a world of flint. Moses lived only last week.

Simon's bees topple about on the 'bloody cranesbill' and the crinkly orange poppies. As for the birds, they are operatic. I should be weeding, but the wildflower meadow says, have pity on these outriders! The weather runs hot and cold. There is spring noise and spring silence. Nothing is in between. Everything is positive.

I do some showy mowing. 'We can see where you've been,' cry the afternoon walkers. I can see where the axe chipper has been – down by our river, in Flintland. Did he sing there? Did he have music while he worked? Did he let the chips fly like the birds? Aeons ahead, an escaped people would sing unto the Lord a new song, for he had done marvellous things.

It is a marvellous thing that Nat holds in his young hands – it is 22-carat something-or-other BC. A master hand had cut it. Poor, tender bleeding flesh at work. Phyllida owns it, and she knows its diamond worth. Countless years later, the Virgin's monograph and the Host would be set in flint on the base of a Suffolk church where I was a warden. This most glorious use, perhaps, was in the flushwork of St Peter and St Paul, Eye. It has been called one of the wonders of Suffolk,

Forever Wormingford

and no traveller should miss it, especially when the sunshine follows rain.

The enormous Garrya looks dead. Yet here and there, in a forest of crisply shrivelling leaves, a little green hangs on. 'Cut it down,' say the know-alls. 'It will come to life again.' But I'll give it the summer. Who could deny it this; and who could deny the twelfth-man ministry of St Matthias, although he is little more than a name? Gaps in factual history are there to be filled with our imagination.

Suffice to say that this lot-drawn apostle was worthy of his rank, else those who had seen, walked with, and heard Jesus, would not have accepted his equality with them. There he is, in the Whitsun room, his presence helping to shake it.

Calling the Banns

THE tall May hedge, which separates me from Duncan, and the twin laburnums, which drench me in gold, are at their mightiest. I should be at the spring weeds, but, of course, I am at the desk, which is heretical. And, on Sunday, careful not to ring the changes too much, I preach on the imagery of the Shepherd and the Lamb.

The cries of new lambs are uncomfortably like those of new humans. Christ identified himself with the good shepherd, calling bad shepherds 'hirelings'. Should there be trouble, the 'hireling runs away because he is an hireling and doesn't care for the sheep'. People work without commitment and can be disconnected from their tasks. It was Jesus's cousin John, down by the river, who, sensing the crowd's mistaken identification of him, pointed to a baptismal candidate and cried out 'Behold the Lamb of God!' 'O Lamb of God,' we pleaded in the ancient village church, 'who takes away the sins of the world, have mercy on *us.*'

'Us' are a score or so of neighbours in the rainy-sunny spring light singing 'The Lord's my Shepherd' and listening to Nehemiah, and to birds outside, and to personal interior voices, or to eloquent silences. Therefore we shall lack nothing. We are not young, we singers of matins, and we lack little but a long future.

The youthfulness of springtime is all too evident. The horse-chestnut by the church gate dances with candles as a chilly wind gets up. Honeysuckles hide the names on Georgian tombs, most of which belong to John Constable's relations. I see them treading blossom as they come through the porch to sing what we are singing – 'And take not thy Holy Spirit from us'. I say some banns. We sing 'We love the place, O God' – and we do. No uncertainty about that.

In my sermon on losing and finding, I include a story about a friend of mine who lost his daughter to the Moonies and who moved heaven and earth to get her back. Only to discover that when he found her, she had to find him – her father – because the sect had wiped him from her memory. Christ is a searcher and finder. The father of his prodigal son never stopped watching for him. And then it happened. The far-distant speck, the dirty tramp of a waster, with the set speech of remorse and guilt. The embarrassment. And then the running father! The homecoming. Faith tells us that recovery or finding must be celebrated.

Some time ago, my neighbour Farmer Brown laid a perfect Bronze Age axehead on my table. It had worked its way up through gravel and chalk, and was 'delivered', as it were, or born again into the utilitarian scene for which it had been made. It was as new as it was when it had left the forge. But what a loss! My heart went out to the pre-Christian loser. I saw him walking and re-walking the hill outside my window at least a hundred times. Or possibly somebody stole it from him after he had purchased it miles away, and they had been too scared to look for it.

In a big old farmhouse, things are lost for ever. There is a conspiracy between it and certain objects. But there is always the certainty that while looking for one thing I will find another. People will say that they are lost for words when they admire something. Like the Queen of Sheba. And I think of the human sound of a lamb in which human being and animal 'speak', as it were. A common voice in the countryside. William Blake heard it.

George Herbert's First Sermon

CALLERS. Expecting a solitary day, I look like the sort of person one should set the dogs on. Bedraggled in my second-best gardening clothes, I am about to mow and weed, edge and admire. First, wise Nigel, to give the boiler some attention; then, a high-born lady with tributes from Waitrose. After which something wonderful happens.

The wintry climate disappears, and, although the sky remains the colour of an old dishcloth, there is the beginning of June warmth. And never such roses! Gloire de Dijon on the house, standards everywhere else. And all out at once. The scent of lilacs. Commotion in the old kitchen. A blackbird beats against an inside window. The beat of its heart against my hand as I show it the door. This is an inside-outside day; a disturbed day.

Forever Wormingford

After lunch, I write letters, and continue to devise a Songs of Praise for the festival of flowers at Mount Bures, from *Hymns Ancient and Modern*, New Standard Edition. The 'mount' of this parish is the tree-covered motte of a castle. Or, more likely, an oaken tower above the River Colne from which to spy on strangers. We have put some nice steps up it, should you wish to see a fine view. Nothing to pay. Stone Age folk sleep in round graves below.

Mount Bures has long been a fine address. For 30 years or more, I have climbed up to it from the Stour Valley to see the wildflowers in its high churchyard, and to touch the closing ring on the door.

I would have preached on Evelyn Underhill this week, but she warrants a preliminary lecture on mysticism. Her book *Mysticism* (1911) redirected the Church of England, and to its astonishment. Her guru was Friedrich von Hügel. They were near-contemporaries. She conducted mysterious retreats, and was one of those rescuers of long-forgotten things that, when found, were seen to be still marvellously bright. What is long unused is often our loss. It is certainly a mystery to me how tiny places, such as Mount Bures, remain permanently fascinating, igniting wonder the minute you step into them.

Rambling about in my books, I discovered, via Izaak Walton, the text of George Herbert's first sermon. It was 'Keep thy heart with diligence', and he chose it from Proverbs 4.23. The sermon itself has long vanished, but I see the tall, sick young poet entering his pulpit, and announcing it in his elegant Cambridge voice to his rustic congregation at Bemerton, he himself having rung the bell for service.

Forever Wormingford

He adored proverbs of any kind, and made a great collection of them. For him, they were concise truths, and things to live by. They cut through the verbiage of politics and religion, through class attitudes and downright ignorance, through legal humbug and sophistry, with their liveliness and deathless wit. He knew, like Jesus with his parables, that there was no forgetting them, once heard.

Once begun on Proverbs, I could read them all day. The Church has notoriously 'skipped' this scripture. Made small use of it – seen it, maybe, as glib. Proverbs in general cut through lengthy statements, and make short work of them. Discourse dreads them. Learning steps back from them. They have been allotted to wiseacres and common folk generally. But they delighted Herbert, the Church of England's finest poet.

Ascension Day

MY TRIPLE calendar comes into use, although I hope not into repetition. It consists of the lectionary, my diary, and my dreams. A kind of knitting together of the days. Thus, on the Ascension, I was young and in Vézelay, but getting on a bit in Wormingford, and in my imagination once again in Dedham Church, staring up at John Constable's gloriously ascending Jesus, which is skied above the north door.

The model was most likely a farm labourer from the Suffolk–Essex border, whom Constable had helped to get a job as doorman at the Royal Academy. Soon, the doorman became a model for the students. He had fought with Wellington, and then, like so many soldiers at that time,

Forever Wormingford

would have been left destitute, had not Constable rescued him.

These homeless, hungry men appear in Dorothy Wordsworth's Journals. This one, because of his beauty, became the Christ of the Ascension.

I vaguely recall having the rest of the day off after the Ascension service. But what I vividly remember was waking up in Vézelay all unsuspectingly to a kind of Ascension riot in the street below. Such shouts, such songs, such clamorous bells! Vézelay was the Burgundian hilltop church where St Bernard notoriously preached the Crusades.

We had arrived there in the dark, so that I was amazed when the shutters were opened wide the next morning to reveal a swallow-soaring heaven and a sacred uproar below. *L'Ascension!* Youthful, laughing priests-to-be lifted their skirts as waiters-to-be watered the flagstones. And there was this urgent calling to prayer from the gold and grey basilica; for, as Mrs Alexander rightly said: 'And ever on our earthly path A gleam of glory lies.'

There is no denying this. Today, as I get started, it takes the shape of a hungry white cat. 'There is no reason to look so glorious,' I say. She has been locked in the larder all night, for some errant reason. The larder was a Victorian pantry, and has a scrubbed brick floor, and a window which squints on to the valley, and enough jam for an orphanage. And wine, maybe, from the slopes of Vézelay. For everything moves on – feasts and songs, recipes and cats.

I preach on the Ascension at another hilltop church, St Mary's, Stoke by Nayland. Constable wreathed it in a rainbow, a sign of harmony, when he painted it during the agricultural riots. Its south doors are thrillingly 'ascensional', in this instance with silver-grey angels in perpetual movement towards God on high.

They crossed my mind as I ascended the pulpit. Godfathers ascend the font here, and make vows on dizzy little platforms: young men, on the whole, who may not have to cling to the font.

A 'cloud of unknowing' took Christ from our earthly sight. When a woman asked Dr Johnson why he had got something wrong in his dictionary, he replied: 'Pure ignorance, madam.' But unknowing is not ignorance, but something contemplative. An unknown medieval author wrote an entire book about it.

He/she said: 'All rational beings, angels and men, possess two faculties, the power of knowing, and the power of loving. To the first, to the intellect, God is for ever unknowable; but to the second, to love, he is completely knowable, and that by every separate individual. This is the everlasting miracle of love.'

JUNE

What Is a Hymn?

JUNE, and Pentecost. I scythe some of the orchard growth to give the Rambling Rector roses a bit of light and freedom. Tied to greengage trees, they have grown apace. Nesting robins fly around in distress; so I give up. I am invasive. In church, the Flower Festival takes over – plus, of course, Songs of Praise. The new priest, John, has a good voice; so has everyone, at this moment. 'Sing out!' I say, encouragingly.

Every year, it is strangely affecting, this ancient building bursting with hymns, the high sills filled with blooms, the scent, the tower clock going tick-tock in the spare silences, the trapped bee or butterfly, the all-too-soon blessing. For, having got into our stride, we should have sung till midnight.

They asked St Augustine, 'What is a hymn?' 'A hymn', he replied, 'is the praise of God by singing. A hymn is a song embodying the praise of God. If there be only praise, but not praise of God, it is not a hymn. If there be praise, but not sung, it is not a hymn. For it to be a hymn, it is needful, therefore, for it to have three things – praise, praise of God, and these sung.'

The hymn-singing faces on the screen, when not over-rehearsed, are holy and absorbed. I sometimes think of the 18-year-old Thomas Hardy at evensong in his parish church.

> On afternoons of drowsy calm
> We stood in the panelled pew,

Forever Wormingford

Singing one-voiced a Tate-and-Brady psalm
To the tune of 'Cambridge New'.
We watched the elms, we watched the rooks,
The clouds upon the breeze,
Between the whiles of glancing at our books,
And swaying like the trees.
So mindless were those outpourings! –
Though I am not aware
That I have gained by subtle thought on things
Since we stood psalming there.

The 'swaying' is interesting. Hardy's continued churchgoing after he had renounced his faith worried his friends. The beat of the Anglican liturgy sets the timing of his great poems. And it still sets the timing of our days for many of us, faint as a heartbeat though it may be. A great or a not very good hymn will set us going, as it were.

When Charles Wesley was in Bristol, he was told about a little girl who dreamed that she had gone for a walk with Christ. 'While we were walking, he said "Sing!"'

'What shall I sing?'

'Sing praises unto the King of this place.'

The summer windows are wide to the dawn chorus. I hear it at about five. Then it stops – like a hymn. Reaches its conclusion.

Grass

A FEW yards to the right, along the ancient road, just before you reach the high-rise accommodation for the mining bees, there arrives, June by June, a paradise of grasses. Not a patch

Forever Wormingford

of grass such as mad kings – Nebuchadnezzar – and mad poets – John Clare – devoured, but a few yards of incomparable grasses.

It is not a sin, however, to know nothing about grasses. Even members of the Wild Flower Society, such as myself, feel little shame in seeing 'grass', and not grasses. Only, it is a pity.

And here, on the edge of the dead rape field, are these tall grasses, each one marvellously distinctive if only I paused to see them. In next to no time, Jonathan, the grim reaper, will be having their heads. But today I will get out my *Grasses, Sedges, Rushes and Ferns* book, and brush up my Monocotyledones/Gramineae; for the residents of this patch deserve homage.

Scripture is full of 'grass', but empty of identity. Its highest use of it is a philosophy for death. Never mind the living glory of my bank: we 'fade away suddenly like the grass. In the morning it is green, and groweth up: but in the evening it is cut down, dried up and withered.'

This imagery was spoken countless times on the lawn-like surface of our churchyard grass, and, somehow, it remains comforting. The grim reaper turns into the natural pastoralist. At home, I mow the long walk, making lines. But under the fruit trees, grasses, sedges, rushes, and ferns grow tall until September.

On the table, some of them plead for identification. 'My name is not "grass", but Great Brome, Orange Foxtail, Sweet Vernal, Bearded Fescue, Darnel, Quaking, Meadow, Bent, Feather, Silky – I could go on . . .'

We have been to St Edmundsbury Cathedral, which is about 24 miles away, to see a kind of grassy, sedgey, rushy children's exhibition. If it doesn't take our breath away,

Forever Wormingford

it makes us wonder. It is both fantastic and yet ordinary, incredible and yet logical. Some notion was sown in their heads, and then they were told to dream on. Is it an oriental view of Suffolk, maybe? One that has to be made before you grow up? And the size of it!

Outside, headstones sink or swim in the great churchyard. Knotty lime trees reach for the sky. St Edmund's dust could be here. He was 29 when he was turned into England's Sebastian. I see him sprawling in summer grass, and watching butterflies, listening to sheep-bells and letting his silver crown tangle with eglantine. The raiders who slaughtered him wanted half-shares in his kingdom, but he had refused. Or it was something like that.

He was our 'river prince', governing the banks of the Brett, Lark, Blyth, Linnet, Stour, Orwell, Waveney, Ouse, etc. Sedges and rushes galore. Mace, taller than him. Water, water everywhere.

My friend David Porteous-Butler has painted Bury St Edmunds, and we look at his pictures. The familiar streets and towers are animate. A pub rocks with young people. Trees admit sunshine. The town glitters, and is both new and ancient, all at once. His palette knife gives edge to the scene. Shall I, I muse, say at the next funeral, 'We fade away suddenly like Sweet Vernal'?

St Barnabas

AFTER a little service for St Barnabas, a favourite of mine, we are off to the birthday party at Suffolk's *Ultima Thule*, Shingle Street. It is where countless stones breed countless flowers,

Forever Wormingford

and the North Sea, when it is in a good mood, becomes an amethyst wall of water.

Everyone we all know is present. The rain has been specially turned off for our benefit. The sky matches the ocean. The Martello tower frowns in the distance. The guests shape their bottoms into the shingle, or sit, good as gold, at round tables. There are cries of joy as people who have not seen each other for at least a month embrace. Never such happiness, never such thankfulness.

And the weather – who could have imagined it? Accompanying our cries there is the coastal din of seabirds, warm wind, and that low hubbub which marks the shore. Old ladies come up and say: 'I'm Diana', and I say, 'Of course!' Leftover Jubilee flags whip from the coastguard houses, and the entire scene is a Dufy watercolour.

The only comparable geography to Shingle Street is Dungeness, and Chesil Beach, in Dorset. Ceosol, cisel, gravel, shingle. But our Shingle Street is by far the ciselest. It descends to the water's edge in ranges of flint mountains that are gemmed with – if you are lucky – amber.

Today, forests of valerian, white and purple, have to be negotiated before our feet sink into a token strip of sand. This is where we East Anglians expected Napoleon and Hitler to arrive. So, in 1808, we took Captain Ford's advice, and built more than 100 Martello towers, from Norfolk to Kent – and, in 1938, no end of pillboxes. But no one came.

Although the towers were 33 feet high and eight feet thick, the North Sea washed seven of them away completely. I feel it looking at us, frail children of dust, as we pass the birthday wine. It sees us as no more than part of the wildlife. It hisses through the countless stones, rubbing them into spheres and

Forever Wormingford

ovoids to the tune of Benjamin Britten's sea music from *Peter Grimes*, and fondles our toes. Oh, frail children of men. But the bright June day, and the 60 close friends – who could better it?

Meanwhile, back at the ranch, I am cutting the grass. It stands tall, and has quite forgotten that it is a lawn. Birds sing tumultuously. I think back to Barnabas, who had to fill the gap left by Judas, and make the round dozen. Twelve was the perfect number. There were not only 12 apostles, but 12 articles in the Peasants' Revolt, 12 great feasts in the Early Church, 12 months in the year, 12 patriarchs, but 13 loaves in a baker's dozen.

Barnabas was a Cyprian Jew. He had the unenviable task of introducing Paul to the eleven. Later on, he fetched Paul from Tarsus, and made arrangements for his first great missionary journey. So, not just a son of consolation, but an outgoing organizer of the infant Church. He was, Luke says, 'a good man'. He is, says the hymn, 'For ever lost in sight.'

This would not be possible at Shingle Street, where one can see a gull at a mile. Clarity, candid and stony, is the rule there. Thick walls, thick jerseys, but never thick heads. It stands on the edge of the sandlings, the ten-mile border of marine Suffolk. It provides not so much a feeling of well-being as of an eternal elation. A human footprint doesn't last a minute.

Mount Bures

'LIVE this day as if thy last,' commands the old hymn. As its author, Thomas Ken, wrote it for schoolboys, one may emphasize its hopefulness rather than its likelihood.

I have always been a fan of the morning, rain or shine. Waking up early, getting up early, is among my treats. I feed the white cat, take tea to guests, do not listen to spoilers such as the News, never watch television, but exist in a kind of tumult of plans and dreams which only chores manage to keep in some sort of order.

And, contrary to Ken's advice, I live the day in the expectancy of a great many days like it, being far too old to 'improve my talent' – or anything else, for that matter.

The garden is heavy with lilac and may, mown grass, and fresh water, the latter pouring without stop to the river. The old rooms are still where once they would have been turbulent with farm children rushing to breakfast and then across the meadows to the village school. The windows are open wide to birdsong.

According to Ken, I should be hearing the night's angels still singing in full voice. And I must 'guard my first springs of thought and will'. Or am I too ancient for this? Or can I not include myself, even now, in the morning's newness? Is not this the secret of living?

Also, I have to create a Songs of Praise service for the Mount Bures fête and flower service. 'No hurry, but if we could have it by tomorrow.' I stay enchanted with this event. With the tree-covered mount, or mott; with the meadows tumbling towards another river; with – I hope – the harebells having escaped the mower. Decade after decade, I lecture the churchyard keeper on the glory of the Mount Bures harebells by the vestry door.

Harebells, *Campanula rotundifolia*, are more pagan than Christian, they say. But never mind. The patch of them in Mount Bures churchyard is a sight to be seen. This, some say, is the bluebell of Scotland. As late as October, the poet John Clare found it in bloom. 'Took a walk in the fields – gathered

Forever Wormingford

a bunch of wildflowers that lingered in sheltered places as loath to die – the ragwort still shines in its yellow clusters – and the little heath bell or harvest bell quakes to the wind under the quick bank and warm furze.'

So it may quake to the wind for ever at Mount Bures – a witch flower, admittedly, but to men, not God. And blueing the turf where the parish buries its priests.

Swallows, and Tom's little plane swoop overhead. But mostly the sky is an enamelled featureless cobalt from an Italian nativity. No hay-making as yet – no activity in any direction. A string of walkers make a magpie descent towards me, then swing north.

I write a sermon on my knee for Wormingford matins, drop off, come to, become bright, grow incoherent, and am reprehended by Ken. 'Improve thy talent with due care.' It is a bit late for that.

My old ash tree groans: 'I shouldn't wonder that I don't fall on your head one of these days.' My neighbours' bees from south and east are ravishing my borders, are classically industrious. I watch them idly. Observance is my occupation, I tell myself.

'Direct, control, suggest, this day,' Ken tells his God. I like the 'suggest'. It leaves room for the imagination.

Scything the Rough

TRY as I might, I fail once again to detach Armed Forces' Day from Remembrance Day. 'There is no Two Minutes' Silence', I tell John. 'One minute then.' But there is, needless to add, Holst. And standards dipping, and 'time like an ever-rolling stream' bearing us all away. Autumn's elegiacs creep into high summer.

Forever Wormingford

I preach a variation on my pacific sermon and, of course, everyone knows what is coming. Medals clink. The door is open, and I can smell hay.

Had I not just witnessed a very different procession, I might have been a trifle dismissive of these rites. But shopping in Colchester, I saw, once again, the funeral of a 19-year-old who had been blown-up a few days ago in Afghanistan. His face, still with the phantom of his childhood present, had looked at me from the screen. Now, with all of us standing still, he passed slowly towards the 'Mayor's' church on the hill. His mum and dad stared at us through darkened glass.

This kind of thing has been going on in Colchester since St Paul set off for Damascus. It is a garrison town and has buried its soldiers from time immemorial. Wrapped up warmly in the Union Jack, a slender coffin is carried into St Peter's, whose bell tolls. The traffic piles up and nobody talks, although faces say Afghanistan. Nobody knows what it means. A woman says, 'Poor little sod.' Which is why I am taking the Armed Forces' Day service as best I can, without trespassing on what has to come.

The elderly colonel, who was a boy in Burma, reads the Sermon on the Mount, in which Jesus insists that his followers are the salt of the earth and the light of the world. To have quenched such a recently lit light. What did they say his name was? His mother will tell us.

I have been scything the rough. Down it falls, five-foot nettles and all. The birds were making a din. The white cat slept on hot bricks. Once a baby squirrel tumbled towards her, but she didn't look up. Every now and then, I run inside to put down a sentence or two, pretending to be a busy writer. As in all ancient buildings, churches especially, the interior strikes

Forever Wormingford

cold. I cut the stems of mint to make tiny jars of sauce, which will see us through the winter. Benjamin Britten is being played on the radio.

I tell lies on the telephone, for where else can they be told, more or less sinlessly? 'The sixth, did you say? I will be in Timbuktu then.' How perfect to go nowhere, to stay in the summer garden, to read in the sun, to hear the waterfall, to smell the roses as well as the hay. A climbing 'Duke of Wellington' scratches the pane like Cathy.

I think of the Colchester Romans looking down at the valley, and out for a nice walk. 'Has this place a name?' 'Not yet, Stephanos. Give it a chance.' They must not be late back, and with the wild garlic from my ditch, because there is to be a memorial service for those who died fighting the Picts, a ghastly lot, white-skinned and bare, with ferocious wives. Pray to the gods that they will never do duty there. I see the Roman walkers lazing away on Duncan's meadow, chewing grasses, half-hoping they will miss all this.

JULY

High Summer

CONSIDERING that the majority of churchyards witness to 1000 years of tears, it is strange that they are so pleasant to visit, to wander in, to sit in on a summer's day. 'Peaceful', the visitors book says over and over again. Peaceful inside and out. 'Do you remember when we threw a tablecloth over that table-tomb and had lunch?' I remind the lady doing the altar flowers.

The sky between the horse-chestnuts is enamelled blue. Opaque. Unseen birds call. Mown or unmown, the English churchyards are green and lively. Georgian gravestones totter, Victorian memorials soar, today's slivers of slate don't know what to say. Albert 'Bert' in brackets. Rarely a biblical word.

I see them still coming up the path, the old ringers, the previous congregations. 'So you've mended the wall!' It loomed out into the lane, and had done so for donkey's years. 'It's the dead having a stretch.' An undefeated spring runs below it, freezing in the winter; so that we slip and slide to our cars.

But not now. It is high summer, the heat fanned by soft winds. Early Trinity, and we are to be clothed with humility. And then comes the scary bit from St Peter, 'because your adversary, the devil, as a roaring lion, walketh about seeking whom he may devour . . .' But the bees swimming in my balsam remind me of the poor dead lion on the treacle tin whose gaping carcase has turned into a honey-pot.

Forever Wormingford

Neighbours move away. We say goodbye in the hospitable house. Already there are gaps where familiar things had stood. 'Oh, but we will often be back – you'll see.' But they won't. Their time with us has ended. They walk round the big room, taking photographs. But the marks on the walls where the pictures have been say everything.

I talk to a gentle, ill man, coming closer to hear his whispering words. Yet there is happiness rather than sadness. A kind of acceptance for things as they are. St Peter, whose week it is, asks God to make us perfect, and to 'stablish, strengthen, and settle us'. But it is unsettling when old friends move away. I mean, where will we go for Christmas-morning drinks? Have they thought of that?

Some have gone to Scotland, and there will be postcards from the white house above the loch to prove it. I see them opening the deer-gates to let the car through, and me waking up in the rare Highland air, and then driving to Ben Lyon.

Perhaps the young shepherd will bring his flock down from the hill, or the Edinburgh minister will be doing holiday duty at the kirk. The shelves of Scottish history will certainly be toppling in the drawing-room. Half a mile from the house, they will encounter Queen Victoria and Mr Brown having a picnic.

Perthshire amazes me – its scent, its indifference to human needs, its vast parishes, its blue ranges which should not have been clothed with pine forests, its stern nobility. Will the pine-marten run along the wall? For we all like to think that the places which have become ours for a week or two possess a perpetuity for us alone.

The white cat has never been to the top of the track. 'Tell me what it is like up there.' Dangerous: bends, haywains with bales, sabbath cyclists, congregations going home, dogs getting lost. She has made her summer bed in the vast stone sink which once stood in the farm kitchen. There she sleeps her nine lives away.

The Prayer Book Society Arrives

THE winter in summer temperature has gone away at last. There is a kind of passion of roses, never so many, and their combined scent collects in the valley.

Windows wide. Two horses are still on the rim of the world. They stand, motionless in opposite directions, just whirling their tails, and will do for hours. When I was a boy, I marvelled that horses, or cows for that matter, tolerated a fence or a hedge. Why they did not jump over them and trot to Bedford, this being for some reason my idea of escape or Shangri-La. It would have made Bunyan laugh.

Stillness is less examined than quietness, about which there are increasing studies. Yet God does not tell us to be quiet. He says that we must be still in order to know him. That, after natural commotion, he will speak to us in a still, small voice. Wordsworth listened to the 'still, sad music of humanity'. Thus the July day, the motionless forest which contains the ancient farmhouse, and Jean's horses without movement shining in the early morning.

The Prayer Book Society arrives. Not all of it, of course, but enough to fill my old rooms. It is youthful and at the beginning of everything, and this is an annual occasion, and one much looked forward to. I am not a member, as I tend not to 'join', being more an apologist. Also lacking the energy of the fully committed, due to seeing round corners, up in the air, etc. Although not at all Laodicean, you understand, but someone with a different fire. Like the horses from the study window. And in any case, we have only got the Book of Common Prayer in our pleasantly backward churches, although our minds are fully awake, you understand.

It is John Clare time. On 13 July, the wonderful nature poet's birthday, I shall give my 31st lecture at Helpston, his native village. And we shall walk the pastures and cornfields where he toiled, and listen to his words in his parish church.

Children will have surrounded his grave with Midsummer Cushions – squares of turf, stuck with wild flowers – and Morris Men will dance outside the Blue Bell pub, and the flatlands of Northamptonshire (now Cambridgeshire) will be curiously hidden and full of secrets, and be both grandly aristocratic and peasant-like at the same time.

As I tell the Clare pilgrims, the majority of us descend from Helpston, from agricultural toil and play. John Clare died in the madhouse in 1864. A signed photo just before this hangs over my head. I look up at it nearly as often as I look out on the towering hill. And now I must re-read him for my lecture and find my way back to his summers.

John Clare's hymn sees Christ as an outcast, and is titled *The Stranger*. He said that, 'The blind met daylight in his eye', and he asks, 'who could such a stranger be?' He listened to the village bell-ringers from the edge of things, along with shepherds and outsiders, along with animals and beings on uncultivated ground. He knew his place. His Jesus was fugitive – 'an outcast thrown in sorrow's way'. Nineteenth-century hymns are full of nineteenth-century grief, pain, and isolation. Clare sings of weeds as much as roses, of flowering ruts as much as gardens. Next door to him were the 'Hills and Holes' from which they quarried cathedrals.

The Curate Is Confirmed

OFF to Helpston for the 32nd time. For John Clare, its native voice, the first Sunday in July was the Helpston feast: 'Wrestling and fighting, the ploughman's fame is still kept up with the usual determined spirit.' Like his contemporary, William Hazlitt, another quiet man, Clare accepts violence in the village. He walks away from it, and into his intellectual world.

> Saw a bird that was an entire stranger to me about the size and shape of a green linnet, and with wings of a brown-grey colour, the crown of the head a deep black that extended downwards no further than the eyes. Went to see Artis [his archaeologist friend] who tried to look it up in his bird book. It was an unnoticed species of the linnet tribe.

Clare was all too noticed for his own peace of mind. A ploughman who wrote poetry? People came to look at him in the fields. He tried to hide – an impossibility in a nineteenth-century village. And now we continue to look at him from all angles.

I read him yet again, before Alan and I set off for what is now the Cambridgeshire border, early in the morning. And there it is, the walled park that cost a pound a yard, the Clare Society, his birthplace next to the pub where he worked, the pleasures of repetition. Although not too much in my presidential address.

Forever Wormingford

The white cat sees us off. For her, the top of the farm track is *Ultima Thule.* Only once in a dozen years did I find her up it, and had to call her back to her own two acres. Meriel the organist is taking her cat miles away, and is dreading it. But long ago some Suffolk friends drove their cat, Holly, to Cornwall, and suffered more than he did. Neither did he recognize me when I arrived, having become Cornish at once.

Today, reading in the study, I watch the horses out of the corner of my eye. One wears a white mask against the flies, the other makes do with her tail. There they stand, deep in horse talk, which is silent.

I have allowed the Himalayan Balsam to riot. It has explosive seeds. Touch their capsule, and they're off. A small child was more disconcerted than amused when invited to do this. Pretty flowers were not supposed to end their lives with such power. The gardener brushing against them with the mower is peppered with seed shot.

What do I say in church in early Trinity? Something I haven't said before, if possible. Shall I read Francis Kilvert? What was he doing on a Victorian July day? He died so young – 39 – and a week after his wedding. His coffin was carried beneath the bridal arch.

William Plomer, the South African poet, published some of his diary in 1939. Amid all the parish duties, there is a longing for girls. It also contains one of my favourite clerical anecdotes.

The curate took his candidate for confirmation when the bishop arrived. They were both youthful and nervous.

'Stand up!' the bishop cried.

'But I am the curate, my Lord.'

'Stand up!' the bishop cried.

Forever Wormingford

So the curate was confirmed.

This was on the Welsh border, you understand.

Such Good Things

DAWN, and I am listening to the third movement of its chorus. Should I rise and shine, or think? Scatterings of this and that fill my head. Queen Victoria used to say that religion made one think of what otherwise one would not think of. I am actually thinking of another hot day. The willows crack in anticipation. The chorus breaks off suddenly into silence. The little stream takes over.

What happened yesterday? I opened the fête in the next village – the one in which Selina, Countess of Huntingdon, opened a chapel for her Connexion. The friend who has been introducing me as the fête-opener now lives in it, and has gravestones in his garden. Lady Huntingdon decided that, as a peeress, she had a right to appoint as many Church of England chaplains as she liked.

She certainly appointed my old friend Gordon's farm to subsidize this chapel. When the Scots came down from Ayrshire before the First World War, they preferred it to the parish church. But the strict Methodists built themselves a tin chapel. It was painted pale green.

But should I get up? These ramblings are unseemly. Also, I can hear the white cat at the door, like a starving man at the gate. The big thing this week has been to keep out the tennis – or much of it. As mother used to say, infuriatingly: 'It is only a game, dear.' The result of such disparagement is that I have never quite learned the rules of any game. But the aesthetic look of the courts – provided they are not filled

Forever Wormingford

with howling ladies – the skill and the beauty of the players, not to mention their ferocity, are a pendant to summer. Like strawberries for breakfast.

They are haymaking at Duncan's. Their little French dog rushes about in ecstasy, and the cry of the girls calling him echoes through the valley.

It is later now, and I am thinking of what to say at the John Clare Festival next weekend. This is my favourite literary pilgrimage. We shall set off at 7.30 for Helpston, once in Northamptonshire, now in Cambridgeshire, and with miles of motorway *en route*. Our East Anglian plaster will turn to Barnack stone. The sky will be different – or appear to be. But Helpston will be the same, as will the Clare followers – a few Japanese; for Edmund Blunden, the great rural poet's first twentieth-century disciple, taught there.

What I like is the way that what is profoundly parochial becomes universal. Like the teaching of Jesus. He took both the language and the wonders of the Temple into the lanes and fields, joining them to his stories, and often on a morning like this, when birdsong fades and a sun like a burning glory rises quickly in the east.

Crowds simmer in the heat, immense gatherings under the sun. I preached on them to a chancel-size congregation. It was cool in church. Four hymns for a matins handful. The collect that says: 'O God, who hast prepared for them that love thee such good things as pass man's understanding', and old, blind Mrs Leach, in her new grave by the door. I had preached on 'crowds' and on blind men in a crowd.

'What do you want me to do for you?'
'Sir, we want our sight.'

Forever Wormingford
The Pilgrimage to Helpston

SULTRY July days. Twin calendars rule them: the lectionary, and a writer's. Thus our trip to Helpston, the birthplace of the great rural poet John Clare. It is exactly as we left it last year, except that a strange additional memorial rises over his grave. Dear once-a-year friends walk along the broad village street, with its handsome Barnack stone houses and towering hollyhocks.

Ringing the changes, my lecture is on Thomas Hardy, whose hands did not touch the soil; and Clare, whose hands drove the plough. Their days slightly overlapped – had they heard of each other? Neither could really operate, as it were, outside their own countryside. In their time, the 'peasant' would become a 'farm labourer', and the bottom of the rural population.

And towards the end of the nineteenth century the British countryside would fall into a depression that would last until the opening of the Second World War, when food needs, and today's non-traditional farming methods, would rescue it from decline.

I looked up Clare's activities in July from his wonderfully useful *The Shepherd's Calendar*. So far as I can tell, virtually nothing happens in Wormingford in July. You might have to squeeze past a hay lorry whose dizzy oblong load totters ahead, and whose driver waves his sunburnt hand. No women semi-dressed in the hay-making fields which so tantalized the young poet. What work does he list for July? Well, mostly anything which meant using a scythe.

I keep my scythe in cutting order with a whet-stone. I bought it in Stowmarket a long time ago, and I am enchanted this moment to see Adrian wielding it in the orchard. Softly, it lays the summer growth down in rhythmic folds. Greengages will tumble down on to them without bruising. You have to beat the birds where there are greengages. A week late, and they will be the debris of a feast.

Clare's July village is noisy with 'singing, shouting herding boys', and bagpipes, as young Scots tramp down the Great North Road to seek their fortunes in London. Our car makes its journey through ancient lanes and motorways to the church at Helpston, where I sit on the chancel step to talk on England's most eloquent village voice, and a prolific one, so that the John Clare Society need never run out of subjects.

We come home to matins and evensong in two different churches, and to the lasting heatwave. Now, with the house empty, and the white cat thanking her god for summer's torpor as she sleeps on the window ledge above what was the copper, I get back to routine, breaking into it now and then to pull up some giant weed. By far my most wondrous July achievement this year is the sweet-pea wigwam: a score of bamboo rods that carry the flowers to heaven. A vase of them locked into a room overnight is the best welcome to a July breakfast.

Clare sees 'the gardener sprinkling showers from watering cans on drooping flowers' as he tended both wild and cultivated plants behind his cottage. It could have been a statement on his own genius. His natural history was marvellously inclusive. It began when he was a boy, lying low in the summer grass, watching climbing insects; and it ended as the beautiful sane region to which he could escape from the 'madhouse'.

Forever Wormingford
St Edmundsbury Cathedral

VISITORS marvel at my hollyhocks. A sumptuous cerise, they sway against the ancient wall. An old gardening book is crammed with hollyhock advice. But I let them get on with it – life. Their buds must have suggested the crockets on spires. They have shabby feet and dizzy tops.

A young Polish neighbour has the grass in hand, and the long walk has stripes. Imagine! Tiny oval Victoria plums nod above it. The white cat searches for shade. Summer rain in the night. It seems to fall for hours, but in the morning nothing is more than damp.

To Bury St Edmunds, to preach on 'The lay voice'. The cathedral burns in the sun. It is full to the brim, and the eucharistic candles waver in an interior freshness. It is just past St Benedict's Day. The true Benedictine asked for little more on earth than to sing in God's house, and to carry the song forward in heaven. The Rule stayed firm and strict, despite the cultural contradictions of history.

Similar to St Francis, Benedict drew the crowds, when all he wanted to do was to exist according to a rule for himself. He was a young man who shrank from anything approaching religious flamboyance. I expect his clever sister Scholastica could have been a bit crushing.

I told the summery cathedral how the Suffolk monks who followed the Benedictine pattern sat in a ring each morning to hear the Gospel read, chapter by chapter, their habits spattered with the blues, reds, greens, and yellows of the windows, while they reaped, as it were, the spiritual harvest of order.

Anglicanism is wonderfully orderly. I sometimes think of poor young John Henry Newman in St Peter's, after he had 'gone over', as they said, as he contrasted its ramshackle processions with those at Oxford. Bury Cathedral on a baking morning would have pleased him. It seemed also full of love and prayer.

It began life as the pilgrims' church – medieval monks were not at all keen to have their place of worship used by holy tramps, and since those at Bury were immensely rich, they were able to build a special church for them. Dedicated to St James, it could hardly have been more beautiful. It waited a few centuries for a tower. All in good time.

Benedict's Rule was not elaborately set to music: it was plainly sung. We lifted the roof. Benedictines share silence. They try not to keep it to themselves. This is an art. Pop festivals share row. But this morning, at Bury St Edmunds, we are to share the lay calling. There is a priesthood of the laity, as well as that of the ordained, and this service at Bury describes it. Neither Benedict nor Francis was ordained.

This coming Sunday, I will read the prayers of Robert Louis Stevenson at matins and evensong, at Wormingford and Little Horkesley. I discovered them in a muddly bookshop years ago, and have come to treasure them. Stevenson wrote them for his 'household' on Samoa, a group of some 40 people.

He summoned them morning and evening by blowing a conch shell, and then, in his fine Edinburgh voice, he would read prayers that only Edinburgh could understand. The Samoans put fresh flowers in their hair, and entered into them in ways that were not to be examined.

'Lord, behold our family here assembled. We thank thee for this place in which we dwell, for the love which unites us, the peace accorded us this day . . .'

AUGUST

John Bottengoms, 1375

WHEN, giving a hostage to fortune, I recklessly announce that I do not take holidays, meaning that I don't have a fortnight in Spain, or Felixstowe, the reply is: 'But your life is all holiday!' So much for the years at the desk.

This country was all holy days until the Reformation, after which you were lucky to get time off for Christmas. Bank Holidays began in 1871, when banks were closed for one day a year. In Thomas Hardy's novels, you got a day off only if some minor mishap – a whitlow on your finger – prevented your working – although, in the old half-dreaming, hard-working countryside, skiving was an honourable art.

As a boy, I would vanish into the long grass, so to speak, to read and escape jobs. As country children, we had our jobs, and mine included milking goats, running errands, and looking after small brothers. I longed to be alone, like Greta Garbo. And now I am – alone with three parishes.

Their wants are part of my happiness, something that puzzles my friends. I have long stopped worrying about repeating myself when I talk to them Sunday after Sunday. Sometimes I read to them, sometimes I teach them. The lesson-readers take such trouble. I could listen to some of them by the hour.

It is Isaiah now, peerless prophet. And a lengthy one, thank goodness. He flourished, as they say, in the eighth century BC. And what a writer! His wonderful book begins with

Forever Wormingford

human desolation, and ends with the new heavens and the new earth. His God tells him: 'Be glad, and rejoice for ever in my creation.'

'I know I should be happy, if in the world I stay,' we sang in Sunday school. Not, of course, on the News, which is as unhappy as journalists can make it: a sad entertainment on the hour. But human nature's balancing propensities defeat such expert gloom, certainly when the sun shines as it does at this moment, hotting up the roof tiles, and driving the white cat under the sheltering leaves.

I am re-reading Virginia Woolf's *The Waves*. 'The sun struck straight upon the house, making the white walls glare between the dark windows. Their panes, woven thickly with green branches, held circles of impenetrable darkness.

'Sharp wedges of light lay upon the window sill and showed inside the room plates with blue rims, cups with curved handles, the bulge of a great bowl, the criss-cross pattern in the rug, and the formidable corners and lines of cabinets and bookcases.' Just as now, this minute. Nothing need be changed in the description. The virtue of such writing is to show us all over again the beauty of the ordinary, the commonplace.

Washing dries between two plum trees. The postman rattles down the stony track. But fewer walkers than in days gone by. It has been a public road since Alfred the Great or John Bottengomes, *c*.1375. It tilts towards the River Stour, with pastures on one side and crops on the other. I know its every flint. They shine in the July sun, just as they do in the spring rain.

The summer birds sing, but I am bad on birdsong, try as I might to identify it. 'But that's a goldcrest,' the old friend tells me, although it will merge into 'birdsong' the minute she leaves.

The Old Testament is terrible on natural history. I learnt some of mine reading the Palestinian information at the back of my Bible during sermons. This when I was a child. I am all attention now, of course. But the summer does make one drift off. It is partly what it is for – meditation.

Church Lavatories and Early English Windows

THE Friends of St Andrew's meet by the river. The Stour fingers its way through the secret reeds. The day has been hot, and now the evening is Mediterranean, with a cobalt sky in which a Chagall moon lies on its back. Unbeknown to most of us, we sit on a purpose-built Saxon mound that keeps the winter floods away.

Some of us have been to the City, and one would have thought that the Friends' finances would be elementary, but what church money has ever been this? And so we put on our thinking caps, as mother would say: other than I, who, financially illiterate, sit in the Patron's chair. And so the evening passes, pleasantly interrupted by salad and wine.

The great debate is, of course, about lavatories and Early English windows. The Vicar, Henry, will not be here to see what happens either way. The comings and goings of incumbents in a rural parish are dramatic, and we will miss him. Unlike artists and writers, he will retire. Our Friends are both retired and still toiling, friends in both senses, beloved neighbours and faraway commuters, and thus the summer night passes. We sit in Essex, Tom's cows munch in Suffolk, and the river passes to make a dividing line.

Forever Wormingford

You can have some yearly fund-raising in a country parish, but not too much fund-raising, which breeds alarm. Not to say exhaustion. A conglomeration of Stone Age and Roman materials, which is also in a kind of everlasting debate on a slight rise, will see us all out, whatever we do or don't do.

But neither we nor the diocesan architects will stand for laissez-faire. We are like little boys with coins in our pockets, who are torn between spending and keeping them there. And thus the gentle argument goes on. And thus my, if I may say so, deep knowledge of village things knows that this will always be so.

The ancient garden is scented. It is where the brass-rubbing knights and ladies in the ringing chamber walked, smelling the same warm air, listening to the late birds, and maybe discussing whether their riches would run to a clerestory. Anything to get them into heaven. Spare no expense!

A Swiss lady has sent me, as she does year after year, a packet of Alpine seeds. They are all in flower, and, although obviously hollyhocks, marigolds, cornflowers, etc., they are smaller and far greater-hued than their English relations. The white cat hides from the sun in their shade. A distant, unrecognizable figure is getting in a bit of hay. The horses stand in profile, flicking off flies. Strangers come and go, and are given a cup of tea.

Peter-Paul the composer arrives to have a talk. We bake against the nettles. How impossible, now, to think of the rain, the washed-away lane, the coldness of only last week. Even of the slugs that devoured my runner beans. At the top, a hare walks, not runs. In church, we sang 'Christ is made the sure foundation', which was rather going it for 17 people. Such a sumptuous hymn; such a glory to match the glory of summer. It rose and fell like the wind-stirred wheat. I preach on the Lord – and the sea.

Later, much mowing, much tying-up of top-heavy tomatoes, much flipping with a book. *Angularis fundamentum* goes on singing in my head.

Our Flower-Show

THE hare does not bolt when we see each other, but takes his time to look at me before lolloping off into the bracken. He is damp and scruffy, and his eyes are like polished stones. He is a sagacious animal, with a thought process that engages with my wonder.

Humanity and hares have a strange history, when you come to think of it, a dramatic way of trying to make sense of one another. We have given hares attributes and plants that have nothing to do with them – and a lot to do with our fantasies. A jack hare with his doe wife and their leveret children do not burrow, but live above ground. The boys box in March.

The Colonel opens the flower and vegetable show, and I award the cups. They have been polished, and stand on black mounts, each with its giver's name lavishly engraved. The Gordon Brown cup, etc. As most of the donors have departed to other rewards, the calling out of their names in the village hall always creates a certain sadness. The Lucas cup, for a single rose.

Long ago, the artist John Nash was being driven by Colonel Lucas's elderly sister, when she nodded off.

'Grace, old girl!'

'Oh, my dear, it must have been the lunch.'

Forever Wormingford

The cricket ground is mown to a T, and, although the temperature is in the 30s, looks cool. A dozen young people do karate, all robed in white like our future selves in the carol. They knock each other over with bare feet. They bow east, south, north, and west when the karate ends. How amazing that they live in our village, and, as far as I am concerned, have been more invisible than hares.

But whereas in my boyhood everything in a village was known, now little is known. And this is not because there is a new way to keep secrets, but because everyone who lives here takes a world-view through the internet, and the car, and has limited interest in parochiality. But this year's flower-show unconsciously releases something that is pure Wormingford — something that no neighbouring village can have, even if it rents the same bunting and marquee, and shares the same goalposts.

I judge the children's handwriting entries. These could not be more minimal. Softly blaring music, gorgeous cake, unloaded paperbacks, the raffle, handsome ladies who have been in the sun, and, at the end, the sell-off of home-made bread and more or less straight runner beans.

On Sunday — Jonah. Jonah for August. His brief tale has been chopped into three, to last out the month. Which is a shame. And, as we all know, like there not being an apple in Genesis, there is no whale. Jonah's notorious three days in the belly of the great fish are really the least fascinating of his adventures.

I like his getting sunburnt as he eagerly takes a grandstand seat above Nineveh — 'that great city' — to watch it burn. God shakes his head. He reminds young Jonah of the divine protection that has been at hand all his wayward life — the big marrow leaf, for example, which now shades him from sunstroke. God says: 'They are not all wicked in Nineveh. Think of the boys and girls, the cats, the cows . . .' We leave Jonah thinking.

Jonathan Mends the Track

SULTRY August, and tall perennials outgrow their strength. I tie up the toppling hollyhocks, and the bees do not chase me as they did the Amorites, but hang on for all they are worth. It is wonderfully still. Motionless. Except, of course, for the bees. William Blake, contemplating their notorious business, said that they had no time for sorrow.

Once upon a time, the work ethic ran amok, but what a disaster it is when it can no longer be practised. When everything has been done. Leisure is leisure only when work calls the tune. 'How doth the little busy bee improve the shining hour?' asked the Taylor sisters, who lived just up the road. But if an hour shines, why attempt to improve it?

Jonathan has improved the far-from-shining track – to the relief of those who travel to Bottengoms – splitting its flints with his machine. And not, I trust, wrecking the home of my beloved mining bees. These creatures apart, bees can be roughly divided into the social and the solitary. Rather like us, I suppose. Rather like the ancient Christian desert-dwellers and monastic communities. Religious choose to live in silence, or within a buzz. Writers tend to have silence thrust on them, even when they have a family.

When a relation came to tea, the dumb telly was the object of her concern for me. 'Is it broken?' She would have driven off to get me a talking one that very minute. Hers talks from

Forever Wormingford

morn till night, and is guaranteed to do so. But, then, so do the bees. The white cat switches on when I am near, and off when I am in the study. August has a summery rumble to it, even before the combines lurch from their sheds. It must be the bees, improving their hours.

In the evening, balsam seed scatters like grapeshot. When I show the children how to encourage this by the gentlest touch of the pod, they scream with excitement, the movement being so strong between their fingers. They find giving a hand to nature quite a nerve. 'Now me!' Balsam flowers, like silk boats, rock above them.

I want August to trail its days and take ages to reach September. Not so parents, I am told. There should be legislation to put boys and girls out of their screen-fed dens in August. There are children in our village whom no one has ever glimpsed. Old commands in my old house ring up the stairs: 'Out, out! Do your chores, then don't come back till teatime. Find another mouse.'

What happened in John Clare's village in August? He is at pains to report it. Although it was in rural Northamptonshire a century and a half ago, it was still rather similar in rural Suffolk between the wars, when I was a boy.

Not that I haven't kept up with change. Or the bits of it that suit me. So this from Clare's August: his publishers had told him to tell the bourgeoisie what country folk did in August: they hadn't noticed. Well, there was no Bank Holiday for them, for a start. Just a lot of hot work. No one was at home. Everyone was in the fields, including:

The ruddy child, nursed in the lap of Care
In Toils rude strife to do his little share,

Forever Wormingford

Beside its mother poddles o'er the land,
Sunburnt, and stooping with a weary hand,
Picking its tiny glean of corn or wheat,
While crackling stubbles wound its little feet . . .

. . . and, I think, on the blazing hill field opposite. Only beyond all memory.

Feet

A FRIEND from Epping arrives to show me pictures of her recently ordained son. He and another youthful deacon walk on either side of the Archbishop of Canterbury. They are clothed in white vestments, but walk to a shrine in bare feet. Their white naked feet tread the soft grass. The vulnerable steps make me think of Blake. My feet are unthinkingly bare at remote Bottengoms, and are hardly ever pierced by a thorn. But the feet in the photograph, due to the robes, cannot but suggest the sacred as well as the natural.

The three men have taken off their shoes and socks at the Walsingham Slipper Chapel, to tread the last mile to the holy place. They smile in the Norfolk sunshine. Temples of all descriptions are barefoot places. The white cat sits in ceaseless adoration of her feet, licking them into shape in the old stone sink. Neither she nor I pick up a thorn. Or rarely ever.

In the shaggy August orchard, which I have begun to scythe, I take note of my badgers' feet as they bumped themselves through the faded grass to the bright stream. At the vet's house above the track, I hear that the sturdy feet of a muntjac and her child beat a hunger march to the kitchen door.

Forever Wormingford

Jesus would complain that he had nowhere to lay his head. But a woman not only bathed, but anointed his feet. The first was ordinary enough, but the second was sensational. Drying them with her hair, she elevated a common courtesy to a sensuous recognition of their walk among us.

One imagines that societies that went barefoot in company would have taken particular care of their feet. More, maybe, than their hands. Naked, they were a form of levelling. And of freedom.

Frightened feet walked in the company of Jesus, all the way from Jerusalem to Emmaus. About seven miles, they say. He, just behind them, then catching up. What I find interesting is that they didn't recognize his step. They had, after all, walked with him for years. But then they had witnessed the nailed feet, whereas the Emmaus Road feet were really stepping it out. So much so that when they all reached Emmaus, it was assumed that the talking fellow-traveller must be worn out.

Had the stranger walked on, he would have come to Gaza, where poor blinded Samson brought the house down on his tormentors. All the walkers would have known this tale. Instead, the fellow walker – removing his sandals, of course – his feet washed but scarred, identified himself in the second eucharist. It was Luke who records this walk, this hospitality. No one else.

The Emmaus Road Christ was to become every Christian's travel companion. His teaching would now for ever be seen as a long walk that was often a trudge, and just as often a stepping-out of place and time. 'Abide with us, fast falls the eventide,' the Emmaus Road walkers said to the talkative stranger who was now in step with them. These are the first

Forever Wormingford

words of the post-resurrection ethos, beseeching Christ to become its guest.

Luke tells another hospitable story about a much shorter walk – to Bethany. And to another hospitality. And to another resting of clean, tired feet. The road-tiredness of Jesus is never left out of history. And then there would be the foot basins and the towels, for the 'beautiful feet'.

The Aftermath

'AUGUST for the people,' said Auden. And the people for the A12. So stay at home, I said.

A little bit of woodland clearing grew into an ambitious amount of nettle-scything and sawing down of some already toppling crack willows (*Salix fragilis*); and by midday I was creating what never in my life had I thought of creating before, a glade. For I saw what the nettles etc. had hidden from me: a perfectly fitted carpet of ivy, and the pearly evidence of disturbed snowdrops.

Thus I toiled all day, virtuous and solitary. The overgrowth had long since hidden a farmyard wall that had kept the animals from straying into the orchard. The white cat, being addicted to walls, observed the emergence of this one with excitement, and, once it had been cleared and brushed down, walked its length rather showily; and, when the 'Suffolk whites' – the somewhat unsettled bricks – had been warmed up by the sun, stretched herself out for the day.

A few of the willows had obligingly fallen far enough for me to cut off their tops nice and tidily before tackling their trunks. By early afternoon, the glade appeared. I prayed that

Forever Wormingford

the August people would not do likewise, would not have what they called 'a run out to see' me, and break into my labour with their Bank Holiday. But they didn't; and by sundown I finished doing what at breakfast had never before crossed my mind. And now I wanted them to see what I had done, so that I could boast.

The following day, I went to Stowmarket to talk about John and Paul Nash and Carrington to the best small U3A group ever. Previous invitations had confronted me with halls full of members of such varying intelligence, if one is allowed to say this, that it became impossible to 'pitch' the address. Here, about 20 women and two men had met twice a month to study art, supplementing the talks and discussions with visits to galleries. It was beautifully manageable, and for the first time I began to recognize the value of this organization.

Stowmarket is one of those partly industrialized East Anglian towns that have always held a fascination for me. It was where my teenage father, plus countless boys from the farm, took their first steps to Gallipoli in 1914. Whenever the Norwich train stops at the station, I look out to see the exuberant throng, scared, thrilled, singing, innocent, by the same cast-iron platform pillars, their homely luggage in piles, their faces tanned from the fields; for it was August for the people.

Driving to the U3A talk, we slowed down to glimpse John Milton's mulberry tree. A visit to his Cambridge tutor, who was now Rector of Stowmarket, was commemorated with its planting. Mulberries and yews live for ever. Both say: 'I was there.'

> God in the whizzing of a pleasant wind
> Shall march upon the tops of mulberry trees,

Forever Wormingford

declared George Peele, a poet Milton would have read but not have emulated. Mulberries should not fruit too near a house with pale carpets, else the floor will look like a recent murder. A single trodden fruit will produce an indelible stain. But the tree itself will last and last, seeing us all out.

SEPTEMBER

To Discoed

AUGUST ended in airy sunshine, and, mercifully, in the début of my dear hornets. Every year, there is a dragged-out absence, and then, suddenly, the annoyed hum as they knock into the lampshades and have to be shown the door. What handsome creatures they are.

Then, a journey to the Welsh Marches. England drops behind, and the western hills come into view, soft in their greys and purples. To Presteigne, that little town on the River Lugg ('light') whose mystery I have never been able to fathom.

It is the Festival of Music and the Arts. A few strings of faded bunting announce that something is going on, but the music! Who would not cross England to hear it? My contribution is a lecture on the potter's contribution to human happiness, given as a sermon in St Andrew's, at the eucharist. We sing 'Christ is made the sure foundation'. It is altogether wonderful; hundreds of voices pouring perpetual melody. I am singing it still, days later.

My host is the poet Edward Storey, whose contribution is to sing the enchantment of neighbouring Discoed, a minute parish two miles away – a shepherd's place, a bird-gathering place, where, from my early morning window, I can watch sheep cropping Offa's Dyke.

Forever Wormingford

These annual excursions are precious. I see and hear many of the same things, but each time differently. And Debbie, who once talked to me about being ordained, will be, in a few days' time, in Hereford Cathedral. She brings me bread and wine. The festival choir sings William Byrd's Mass for Four Voices. It threads its way into countless subconsciouses. All these visitors! Although here and there a recognizable Presteigne face.

At the end, each of us, ungratefully, describes ourselves as a 'pilgrim through this barren land'. In my sermon, I describe God's asking each one of us: 'My beautiful world – why didn't you enjoy it more?'

Home, through what should have been the Bank Holiday traffic. Only there wasn't any. Just a long run on sparse roads. And Bosworth and Naseby battlefields under our tyres. In my frequently hopeless way, I take a wrong turn, and we are in a mesh of sunken lanes. They are worth the confusion. Signposts point to the most unlikely destinations. How curious it is to hear them singing 'consubstantial, co-eternal'. The Essex countryside, in particular, newly harvested and looking too tempting merely to drive through, and, of course, full of song. Even my old farm-track added a few notes. Four horses in Lower Bottom lifted up their heads.

But in the late-summer garden, nature had better things to do. Taught by my betters not to cut down plants the moment they start to seed, I touched the impatiens balsam, and felt the thrilling push of the pod between my fingers. I was a child again. Its contents flew. Life! That is the thing.

I scythed part of the orchard so that its seed fell into that furry darkness in which fruited trees are rooted, and made a proper step between August and September. The white cat climbed to the topmost branches and gazed down. Greengages were on the turn. And still the Presteigne eucharist rewound itself and played all over again. And the quietness of the Presteigne streets took over the noisiness of the Bottengoms lane, now that all my hornets were bumping their way into the grapevine.

The Least of the Apostles

SUMMER rain – warm, drenching. It catches me up before I can get to the house, a familiar sensation since boyhood, briefly a plight, then a pleasure. The rain it raineth every day, but only a little. Not like today, when it is as continuous as Portia's mercy. It pours through a break in the guttering, it streams through the oaks, it makes an extra river in the farm track.

Thomas Hardy made it fall with a wounding splash on poor Tess's new grave, as if what had happened to her wasn't enough. And his field-women, soaked to the skin, cried 'How it rained!' But, seeing it through the window, all I can do is to meditate on its soft, remorseless progress, watch the plants bend before it, and the valley itself receive it.

On Sunday, Paul calls himself the least of the apostles, because of what he had been. The past weighs heavily on him, especially his ignominious taking care of the coats of those who stoned Stephen.

Also, hundreds of Christ's followers had witnessed him as the resurrected Lord, but Paul had not. He felt it as a deserved and indelible reproach. Yet by grace he was what he was, and not what he had been. He had toiled for Jesus more than all the others put together; so this grace was more than their

Forever Wormingford

grace. It validated his apostleship – it gave him the right to be what he was, and to say what he did. Not to mention the beauty of his expression.

Where did he learn to write? In that far from mean city, Tarsus? Or, as with many great writers – Shakespeare at Stratford grammar school, Keats at Enfield – had there been a minimal of 'learning'?

There was, of course, the proud dual nationality, and the confidence which came from it. But how much of this would have come down to us had he not been locked up? Oratory then being a formal part of education, he would have lectured more than write letters. These bring us close to him. Those to the Romans, whether Jews or Gentiles, are tenderly inclusive. Those to all the other churches recognize their particular countries, but without description; for being one in Christ, not in nations, is the true unity of men.

On Sunday, I climb into Wormingford pulpit, and say what I must have said before, but it cannot be helped. And the dear neighbours sit where they have sat for years. And the medieval arches soar overhead, and St Alban, in his Roman tunic and sandals, looks across the red altar.

And Christopher plays his introit. And one candle wavers, and the other doesn't. And we sing 'Morning has broken like the first morning', and I remember Eleanor Farjeon, who died in 1965, which is yesterday in Anglican terms.

Coming home, walking through the orchard, the Victoria plums touch my head. And the sculptor Jon Edgar writes to ask if I think that his clay bust of me should be turned into bronze.

I look at myself from previously impossible angles, and myself looks back at me. I have irises, not the blind gaze of classical heads – although they were not blind to begin with, the painted eyes have faded, then gone. Lashes, too. Now this marble stare. This seeing nothing and this open-to-everything look. Did anyone think of repainting the pupils of ancient statuary? What a sensation!

Pupil, the dark aperture at the centre of the iris through which light enters. The impatience of Jesus. 'A little while the light is with you. Walk while you have the light.'

Applause

HUMAN hollering is in fine voice. People are paying good money to shout. And now the American election roars away. What do other creatures make of it? I put this question to the white cat, no one else being around. She answers it with her exquisite silence. Stadium sound is historic. One must include the House of Commons in this, and also, most pulsatingly, Welsh rugby.

For me, it has always been voices off. The Olympics have raised yelling to the heights. I cannot imagine joining in – although one never knows. To reach our town cemetery, I have to cross the Roman amphitheatre, where 20,000 ticket-holders, they tell me, once hollered for all they were worth.

The garden, too, is unruly, since it is mid-September. It is doing what it likes. The old seat grows moss, the beds anything they fancy. Sweetpeas rise above it. Such scent, such quietness. But convolvulus, too, climbs whatever happens to fade beside it: hollyhock stems, seedy daisies, a gaunt rose. We all need something to hold on to.

Here, it is pick-your-own blackberries. A big bowl of them raw for dinner, plus cream. I whet Roger's scythe, and lay the orchard grass low. The immortal rise and fall of all

Forever Wormingford

things – what a relief to know this. At village funerals, I omit the skin worms, but never the grass in Psalm 90. The words are so beautiful that it is almost worth dying to experience them. When one is very old, one passes through medicine to philosophy, and through faith to acceptance.

Speaking of passing, what a lot one misses by not taking a turning. Last Sunday, we turned off the familiar Cambridge road to a handful of parishes that were as new to me as some territory in the wilds of Italy. Villages with lovely names: Weston Colville, Westley Waterless.

We had come to pay homage to a rustic poet, James Withers, and in his own church. Twin elderly sisters had arranged wild flowers in it. Deep lanes in undulating fields. Late sunshine. Evensong, perfectly, although a little uncertainly, sung. Intercessions with profound pauses from the back. All as it should be.

I spoke from the pulpit on John Clare, the finest of all village voices. And read his nightingale poem to the most apprehensive of birds. In it, a boy longing to see its nest creeps through the undergrowth, nearer and nearer to where it sings; not like John Keats's nightingale, in palaces, but in a thicket.

> How curious is the nest. No other bird
> Uses such loose materials or weaves
> Their dwellings in such spots: dead oaken leaves
> Are placed without, and velvet moss within,
> And little scraps of grass – and scant and spare
> Of what seems scarce materials, down and hair . . .

A funny year for fruit: almost no Victoria plums; tiny blackberries; few apples. But, surprisingly, considering the rain

Forever Wormingford

and the last-minute sun, pretty good corn. And now this hot September, with novels and a drink on the wobbly garden table, and giant convolvulus winding its way up Duncan's generator to the stars.

The Potter

A MONTH of sun and a day of rain have made the climbers take liberties. The grape on the Vermeer-like south wall has taken a leap to the Garrya, and made a curtain of leaves and fruit. Writing an introduction to William Golding's novel *Close Quarters*, I am shot at by balsam seed. Somebody mows the baked lawns. Roof-high roses fall.

So Seamus Heaney has died. A farmer's son. He wrote like a man who could thatch a stack. And early September would have suited him. Famous Seamus, they called him. They said that he liked John Clare. Field poets touch hands in September, I like to think. The ripening world will be missing him.

September should be busy, but, like all the other months, there is little doing. Birds make music patterns on my telephone wires, and the Proms crash away on the box. All that sound, and not even the white cat giving ear. But that is how it is when the sun shines. I pick a Victoria plum in passing. My little tomatoes hang 20 to the bunch. In the Book of Common Prayer, after the Thanksgiving for fair Weather, there is one for Plenty.

Plenty is manifest in my garden at this moment. How shall I eat it all? Instead of building bigger barns, as in the parable, I must buy a bigger freezer. Or, better still, give some Victorias to the postman. The air is intoxicating – motionless scent.

Forever Wormingford

Bees and cabbage whites cling to stamens. Although, here and there, a faint thinning-out points to later days.

What shall I say on Trinity 15? On the Welsh border, I philosophized on the potter's art. So perhaps this, once more. In Chronicles – St Jerome gave this Old Testament book its name – potters came first. You ate from clay, and your dust rested in clay. I imagine that those poor men having a last supper with their Lord drank passover wine from a pottery cup, and not from a jewelled grail.

The miracle now is that pottery lasts. Fragile though it is, and eminently breakable though it is, it can remain whole for thousands of years. The woman at the well would have filled up a tall pot and departed with it on her head.

Humanity becomes mere pottery in Edward FitzGerald's *Rubáiyát of Omar Khayyám*. FitzGerald says that although the pot has been thrown by the divine creator, given the choice, 'Would we not shatter it to bits and then mould it closer to the heart's desire?' Some do, of course, although the plastic surgeon is no potter.

Singing opposite me in church is our famed potter, Brenda Green. It is not all hands to the potter's wheel, only skilled hands such as hers. The shining wet clay rises as it spins, delicate as the flesh that contains it, as does bread. And, like bread, it must bake. Bread and clay join for that first 'Do this in remembrance of me.' And, originally, for every meal.

They said that Magdalen Herbert – George's mother – often laid a place for Christ at supper. At the altar, I hold up the thin silver cup that has been sipped in our church since before Herbert. The soft lips, the worn hands, the sacred moment, the bowed heads, the wandering hymn.

Forever Wormingford

Sweet sacrament divine,
Hid in thine earthly home . . .

Lancelot Andrewes

UP AT dawn, more or less, the great end of summer sun spinning along the top field, the girls luring their horses, the day promising. Visitors come to look at the garden. Ash leaves float down on our heads, wilting hands above and below us. We tell each other the obvious, that the birds have left, that the frost is to come.

There is the familiar pleasant smell of decay. And sticks everywhere, waving seed about and perfect in themselves. Never give a garden a tidy too soon. Allow its gauntness. Observe the lesson of its passing. Let the grass grow under your feet for a while. Be patient, be thoughtful, be philosophical if you can.

What does the lectionary say? Lancelot Andrewes. He taught George Herbert and a straggle of Westminster boys as they walked along the Thames path. A wonderful teacher to open the autumn, this being a contemplative time, so who better. Andrewes had arrived at Westminster as dean four years before Herbert had arrived as a pupil, and had transformed the place. His Christmas and Easter sermons were earth-shaking. He was on Isaiah, learned, simple, complicated, and thrilling as he re-told the tale of redemptive love. George Herbert, a tall lad trudging along, would have found the mixture of fresh air and fresh Christianity, sparkling beyond words.

Only it was the language itself which intoxicated body and soul. He would later confess that:

Forever Wormingford

I know the ways of learning; both the head
And pipes that feed the press, and make it run

The press had just produced the King James Bible. Dean Andrewes, striding ahead on the Thames path, was making its beautiful words 'run'. The dean prayed for his pupils thus:

The Youth among us,
Students in Schools,
Those under instruction,
Children, Boys and Youths,
Charge formerly or now.

As a schoolboy in Andrewes' class, George Herbert found himself not only at his desk, but also in music's 'house of pleasure' and at the entrance to 'heaven's door'. So are so many of us when, sightseeing, perhaps, matins and evensong are sung. The Japanese tourists and the rarely attending church visitors, other than to carry a Pevsner and not a prayer-book to the altar, are given pause as the same words which George Herbert lived by travel through the Gothic space.

A window for him was designed in 1876. He shares it with William Cowper. Herbert stands at the Bemerton church porch, Cowper in his dressing-gown in his Olney garden, with hares at his feet. The poet is gazing at the portrait of his dead mother and saying sadly:

Oh that those lips had language! Life has passed
With me roughly since I heard thee last.

Herbert is blessing his parishioners as he tells them:

Forever Wormingford

If thou do ill, the joy fades, not the pains;
If well, the pain doth fade, the joy remains.

Autumn for a remaining joy.

The Freshness of Repeated Actions

BLESSED routine. No appointments in the diary, thus a full day. Blessed Lord, grant thy servants the inestimable joys of routine. Blackberries for breakfast. They have to be eaten up before it's October and they get spitted. I wander about in the soaking orchard, a bedraggled sight. Pale hay where I have begun to scythe, brittle seeding-plants everywhere else. No fruit to squash in the long grass this year. But blackberries galore. My badgers have made a highway from the field edge to the stream. The stream has cut Wormingford off from Little Horkesley for ever and ever.

'But it is a united benefice,' I tell it.

'Whoever heard of such a thing?' the stream replies.

The Bishop is coming to see the Vicar off, routinely but lovingly. I shall hold his crozier and hand him his mitre. Each of them has mastered the art of routine – of retaining the freshness of repeated actions. Now what shall we do? Interregnums may be routine, but each one of them is a space that is not at all like its predecessors.

Henry's leaving present is a hefty garden seat that our village joiner has made from the immense old fir tree that swayed dangerously near the tower. It was planted by a priest in the 1890s. The remainder of it is blazing on our hearths. Simon, our woodman, brought it down.

Forever Wormingford

All around, the Suffolk – Essex fields are in different stages of clearance, full cultivation – for the supermarkets – and rest. They are also full of birds, and are lit morning and evening by glaringly beautiful suns. The sky becomes an aerial goldmine of exposed seams, and a vision of the insubstantial. Our vicarage is the grandstand for all this. But my old farmhouse knows only golden mornings, and has never in all its centuries witnessed sunset. All its routines have taken place in broad daylight. And at dead of night.

There is no more compulsive routine than that followed by the true diarist. Diarists are frank about this. James Boswell admitted that he could live no more than he could record. And the self-indulgent Anaïs Nin declared: 'The period without the diary remains an ordeal. Every evening I want my diary as one wants opium.'

For me, the diary of diaries was written by a young curate on the Welsh border, Francis Kilvert. So what a marvel that they found the family photograph-album to illustrate it. As president of the Kilvert Society, I give myself leave to pore over this black-and-white Victorian Church of England heyday. To identify the serious faces, the 'caught' tennis matches, the assembled college students, and the handsome person of Kilvert himself before death carried him out of sight, aged 39.

'Why do I keep this voluminous journal?' he asked himself. 'I can hardly tell. Partly because life appears to me such a curious and wonderful thing that it almost seems a pity that such a humble and uneventful life as mine should pass altogether away without some such record as this.'

The routine of uneventfulness, this is what I praise in the early-morning orchard. Of Jamie the postman bumping down the track. Of the swerving flight of the green woodpecker. Of the white cat cleaning her chops on the wall.

Liturgy

THE classic September days take their time as they succeed each other. No hurry. They are turning Old Master-gold. Come out and do nothing, they say. A nine-month-old baby calls and bumps about on his bottom, talking in Czech and English, but it is all double Dutch to me. He lives in the Barbican. High up? Low down? Is there grass? 'Oh, yes.' I have only his parents' word for it. His round blue eyes shine.

The white cat lies on the garden wall, taking it all in. Chiffchaffs talk monotonously in their thicket; otherwise the late summer quietness prevails.

Alone, I call my sloth 'meditation'. The postman brings proofs of an essay I have written about Laurie Lee, something that has to be read without reading, as it were, so as not to miss a mistake. I pick up falls in the orchard: Victorias, apples – the latter are fit only for the birds, but the plums are bursting and delicious. And too many to devour at this stage; so I put them into plastic bags for the fridge.

Coming down to make the morning tea at six, I encounter a Miss Muffet-size spider attempting to climb the sink Alps, and carry him to the doorstep. I always mean to study spiders, but there is so much to do, so little time, as they say. But I am discovering a method of sorting out small blocks of time for this or that, although the lectionary is no help.

A long time ago, I read the wrong Trinity collect, and, at the door, a farmer's wife said that it had quite spoilt her

Forever Wormingford

worship. I nearly replied, 'I don't believe you', which I didn't, but I thought better of it, and looked contrite, even wicked.

We had a Church of Ireland priest who had the Bible borne before him on a red cushion as we processed in, which I thought most beautiful; but she did not. 'It quite spoilt my worship.'

Little spoils mine. The centuries of words and music and silences keep me on the illimitableness of what might happen during a country service. 'I spy strangers,' we all say, should such grace us with their presence. From my seat, I watch some of them blundering their way through the Book of Common Prayer, others helping. 'Lord, we beseech thee to keep thy household the Church in continual godliness . . . to the glory of thy Name.' Both in and out of the building there is our inescapably grand history, our wildflowers, our views.

David arrives to split up the willow logs that he cut last winter. They tumble musically as the axe falls. He builds them into shining walls inside the old dairy. It is impossible to feel what the coming cold will be like. But 'sufficient unto the day' etc., Jesus said. 'Don't look back: remember Lot's wife.' And don't look forward: live for today.

Children always look forward, and have no idea about living for today. Who would, with so much to look forward to, and maths to be solved before tomorrow? I like to read old diaries to find out what Parson Woodforde, for example, was doing in his Norfolk parish at this time of the year. Eating, of course; but what else?

> 10 September 1783. 'I walked to Church this morning and publickly baptized Mr Custance's little Maid by name Frances Anne. After I had performed the ceremony, Mr Custance came to me and made me a present of 5.5.0 wrapt

Forever Wormingford

up in a clean piece of Paper. We stayed up at night till after 11 o'clock on account of its being a total Eclipse of the Moon.'

That evening, he had lost nine shillings at cards. Turkey and a goose for dinner. The Bishop of Norwich affable. A single parish. Two cheeky servants.

Quarter Day

THREE days before Michaelmas – farmers' quarter day. Warm sunshine, Victorias squishy underfoot, sweet decay in the air. The harvest all gone, its stubble all ploughed in. The first ash leaves sailing down. The ducks in rowdy echelon overhead. Everything as it was and as it should be.

The Friends of Essex Churches arrive in ours to hear me talking about John Constable, a local boy. His mother would write:

> My dear John, I was much pleased with the attention and intention of your intelligent letter, by this day's post; the milk of human kindness is to me an exhilarating cup, and most delightful admixture . . . besides being so cheap and easily given . . .
>
> The account you give of your best love and our great favourite is most grateful, and my wish and prayers are that I may be permitted to see you both happy and rewarded according to your deserts.

Her son has fallen in love with Maria Bicknell. It is the midsummer of 1812. They would court on the Langham hills, the youthful artist being considered a fortune hunter by her

Forever Wormingford

family. John would be walking to Wormingford Hall, which his uncle had rented from the squire, Mr Tufnell.

They say that there are many more trees in the Stour Valley than then. There would certainly have been many more harvesters – the two-legged kind. Only David in his combine, now, and he so furtively that I missed seeing him. Just his fresh ruts.

But three harvest festivals when Jesus walked Palestine, eating an ear or two on the way. How disgraceful. Call yourself a prophet? Phyllida will save a whole sheaf from her fields to put up front at harvest festival. Today's village can only cope with symbols, not with toil.

You have to be old to have lifted a stook. They were surprisingly weighty and prickly. Once they had been carted to the stack yard, the field would flower for a month or more with what we called the aftermath – second shootings of corn and scarlet pimpernel. Belated poppies and scabious.

The aftermath was a study in modesty. Also a country walk. We are in a Stone Age settlement; so I search the aftermath for artefacts, and the study window-sill is crowded with worked flints.

It is the eve of St Michael and All Angels, and Christopher and I are in Fordham Church to hear a piano recital. As always, my attention is disturbed by history, and Mendelssohn and Ravel have to fight for precedence against such claimants as the once-occupier of the Lady chapel, medieval carpentry, and the new west-end gallery.

But the youthful pianist soon drives away these sideshows. He plays Mompou's bell music in a landscape of church bells. He was walking in Paris with his girlfriend when they heard the midnight bell. Our bells sound up and down the Stour, according to the wind.

Coming home, the car lights disturb the Little Owls that live in the sloe bushes above the farm track. They wing around indignantly. Humans have no business being abroad at such an hour. One of the Mompou pieces was called 'Carts of Galicia'.

OCTOBER

John Betjeman's Felixstowe

TO FELIXSTOWE, named after Felix of Dunwich, not to be confused with the 67 other Felixes in the martyrology. Wild weather. The polite seaside town where we paddled as children is now a European base. Massive vehicles with names in double Dutch crowd our little car. Their drivers look down on us haughtily. To think that our Felix Christianized us from these sandlings! Was it our shortcomings that brought them from Burgundy?

The October trees burn, fired up by autumn. We lunch on fish pie. The North Sea is neatly ruled from the firmament, and balances a little boat on the horizon. Yachts are laid up for the winter. The stony beach rattles. All is as it was – airy, harsh, bright.

Felixstowe brings to mind that touching poem 'The Last of Her Order', in which John Betjeman observes a devout old Sister making her way to holy communion. Seaside towns are studded with places of worship – some barely breathing, like that in the poem. Young clergy try to rouse them from their slumbers with clapped hands, startling the retired, some of whom would give their souls for a bit of Merbecke.

Grand hotels have been turned into flats. But tennis thrives. I can hear my cousin Winifred playing for Suffolk.

Forever Wormingford

The turbulent October air hurls us along with promises that we shall live for ever. In Felixstowe, of course.

It is *Beowulf* land: a stretch of Scandinavia discovered in East Anglia – dreadful people, really, all mead and bloody swords. I hope they paused now and then to see the leaves turning. Their deeds come to us in the finest Old English. And just after breakfast.

Seabirds wheel around. It is supposed to rain, but a fierce sun cuts the sky into gold bars. Golfers have turned up in their hundreds, according to the cars outside the clubhouse. Play is now a large part of existence for many people – playing, and watching.

And the Felixstowe lady in the poem kept prayer going. I heard that the churchwardens in a seaside church were now dubbed 'greeters'. One of the most tender welcomes I ever received from a little congregation was when old hands brushed the rain from my coat as I entered a Welsh church. It was pouring and quite a walk from the car, the bell speaking its final notes, and I was drenched. My companion, too. There we were, being received, touched. And the lovely, unknown-to-us hymn. And the clatter of the storm on the roof. Everything the same, yet 'different'.

It is a great year for orchards. For falls. Although mind your heads when it comes to my Warden pear. This is a baking pear, said to have been prized by the Cistercian monks of Wardon, Bedfordshire. The artist John Nash planted it at Bottengoms. Henry IV ate it at his wedding, when it would have been served with venison, quail, and sturgeon.

There is no hope of picking it from my tree, which stretches to heaven. Too hard to bruise, it falls into the dying grass. Warden pies were all the rage.

Forever Wormingford

The Canon sigh'd – but, rousing, cried, 'I answer to thy call,
And a Warden-pie's a dainty dish to mortify withal!'

I stew it gently in its rough skin with cloves and sugar. It is a most distinguished fruit, which a sudden gale is bringing down. A fifteenth-century recipe says cook it with fish – with anything you like. You will need a strong knife and a strong wrist.

Colchester Boy

A WILD October morning. Bottengoms is calm in the front and tempestuous at the rear, where the trees I planted a lifetime ago meet the sky. Leaves race past. Birds protest. Or maybe they are simply exultant as they are blown about.

Tidying a bookshelf, trying not to read, I am taken back by the scent of an ancient volume to Archbishop Samuel Harsnett – that local boy made good. In a niche in Colchester Town Hall I sometimes look up to him as an autocratic priest who takes his place among our worthies, but for me was little more than a Proustian odour, until I decided to find out why he was there, high above us in his robes and Lambeth hat.

The closest I got to this Archbishop of York was polishing his books. They had been buried in tea chests during the war in case Hitler got hold of them and became an Anglican. There were some 800 volumes, including Caxton's edition of Boethius's *Consolation of Philosophy*, and their leather covers had to be rubbed with a foul preservative that the British Museum had recommended. Some of these books had belonged to Luther and other Reformers.

So I sat, day after day, in the Harsnett library, polishing them up, now and then catching some spidery hand, perhaps

Forever Wormingford

of the Archbishop himself, as it descended in the margin. And now, in my old house, a tumble of books releases this preservative smell.

Who was this Harsnett – apart from being the owner of these volumes? Who was he, apart from being a famous local boy? Just up the road, in Ipswich, another local boy had become Cardinal Wolsey, and he an Ipswich tradesman's son. Wolsey loved a bit of pomp. He built Hampton Court Palace, and was very nearly Pope.

Alas, it all tumbled down – not Hampton Court, but the dizzy height itself. Wolsey was on the road when he heard of it, sick, perched on a mule, glad to be taken in by monks. 'Had I but served my God with half the zeal I served my King . . .', he murmured. And what of the college that would bear his illustrious name, in Ipswich? It would get no further than the gate.

Archbishop Harsnett and Cardinal Wolsey, now a stack of sticky books, and another local boy polishing away. All that vellum – calfskin; all those frontispieces on which the deity shared space with lordly churchmen.

But I have become fond of Harsnett. He was not an easy person. He founded Chigwell School, which continues to grow apace. But, although he himself had abandoned what he called the painful trade of teaching, he licensed books for the press. Once, he licensed a book without reading it. But if it was anything like some of the books in his own library, whose slippery covers I was polishing, I could sympathize.

These days, a new book smells good. Often, when I buy one, I open it at random, outside the bookshop – a novel, perhaps, or a collection of poems – and the essence of what is in it reaches my nose before it finds its way to my brain.

Forever Wormingford

The great publishing houses have hardbacks that possess a distinctive scent. Not so with paperbacks, although those that one can buy in church porches reek a little of abandonment, of never being loved. The other day, a pressed flower that I had picked in Scotland fell out of a book. I returned it to its tomb in Dylan Thomas's poems, where it marked no particular place, but had left a small stain.

Now we have put the clocks back, and brought reading forward. I bank up leaves in the garden. They are mountainous, but they will rot down, blacken, smoulder, given a chance. Below them, a cold stream hurries to the river without a pause, brighter than any old book could ever be.

Michaelmas Wakes

OCTOBER is when one has to seize the moment. Sunshine one day, wild rain the next. So far, not a falling leaf. A good mow pulls the garden together. I steer round stands of naked ladies (*Colchicum*, from Colchis, the country from which the Argonauts set out), and islands of white and pink cyclamen. There is a fine crop of old roses. Owls hoot in the daytime. Nettles flag. The white cat watches me from on high – a walnut tree from which squirrels have seized all the fruit. Six horses are in silent conversation on the hilltop. It is a very nice, mild day, but it will not be like this tomorrow.

Although it is autumn, St Mark's urgency fills my head. He is worried that his words might be wasted in short-lived cults. He is young and vital. He knows that here and there, patchily though vividly, what he is saying will survive, will grow, will mature, will change the world. So he tells it his brief Keep Awake parable.

Forever Wormingford

'Be alert, be wakeful. You do not know when the moment comes. It is like a man away from home: he has left his house and put his servants in charge, each with his own work to do, and he has ordered the doorkeeper to stay awake. Keep awake, then; for you do not know when the master of the house is coming. Evening or midnight, cock-crow or early dawn – if he comes suddenly, he must not find you asleep. And what I say to you I say to everyone: keep awake.'

I have been to Wales to talk about my days with Benjamin Britten, who will be 100 years old very soon. Now there was a lively man. Roger, Lucilla, and I drove through the Midlands to Powys in moody lovely weather. Here and there we noted chasing poplar leaves. The skies shifted from the theatrical to the plain dull. Countries smell different. The Welsh border has a distinct odour which is not at all like that of East Anglia, although what it is exactly one cannot put into words.

At Discoed, a minute parish near Presteigne, the poet Edward Storey had 'produced' the last of his Michaelmas Wakes – the smallest and most enchanting of festivals. In a decade he has revitalized an ancient shepherd church on the edge of Offa's Dyke. A yew tree as old as Abraham tells of an earlier faith near by. For ten years, I have listened to it from the bathroom window.

Once in Wales, I don't want to return. I long to go deeper and deeper into the soft hills, to enter sunken lanes made by countless sheep, and men who have left no name, only the marks where they have walked. At Discoed, it is perpetually autumn.

Coming home, we have Michaelmas goose for lunch in a rambling pub – Sunday dinner. Dogs and children. A smoking log. No fuss. Huge rooms. It is where the poet Edward Thomas might have put his feet up on one of his literary walks. Before this, the three of us found a little church about to have pre-harvest-festival communion, and sat behind a good-as-gold family. There was a stately screen and a glorious roof. And a tall priest with green vestments. He stood under the screen and preached on prayer.

Eventually, we came to Cambridge, and then to Bottengoms Farm. Where the white cat still sat where she was when I left – fed and watered and loved, I should hastily add, by servants who stayed awake.

Weather

THE classic rainy day: the sky a liquid colourlessness, the trees drenching sieves, the farm track a river, the fields just dull and wet. The old labourers 'saved' for such a day because, unable to work, they would not be paid. Four horses soak it up, the streaming day; whether indifferent to it or enjoying it, who knows?

Cocooned in the old house, I have to settle down to it as it rattles the windows and surges through the guttering. Fieldwise, it could not have come at a better time. October was dry as a biscuit, and the dusty winter wheat had been aching for a shower; but this downpour! It is not unlike Australian rain. One minute I was baking, the next drowning. No point in running for shelter. In any case, it had been thrilling: the heat suddenly all washed away, and oneself as wet as a surfer.

The Duke of Norfolk's magnificent tomb in Framlingham Church has a Genesis frieze that includes Noah's Ark. Benjamin Britten liked to take children to see it. He turned it into one of his Church Parables, *Noyes Fludde*, with a marvellous setting of 'Eternal Father, strong to save'. I remember singing it for the first time in Orford Church, long ago. William Whiting wrote

Forever Wormingford

it for *Hymns Ancient and Modern*, in 1860. Britten's version is heartbreakingly plaintive, slow, and sumptuous.

He would have seen the memorial to a Victorian crew in Aldeburgh churchyard, and would have more than once witnessed the lifeboatmen launching their new boat to rescue some vessel, maybe some holiday yacht that had not understood the North Sea's power: from being leisurely, it had become imperious, throwing craft and men about like toys. We lesser mortals watched. Watching is a coastal profession. Also a Christian imperative.

St Matthew reports Jesus as saying: 'When it is evening, you say, "It will be fair weather; for the sky is red." And, in the morning, "It will be stormy today; for the sky is red and threatening." You know how to interpret the appearance of the sky, but you cannot interpret the signs of the times. An evil and adulterous generation seeks for a sign, but no sign shall be given it except the sign of Jonah.'

Jesus refers to this sign more than once; so what is it? That he will be returned to life and not swallowed up? The island nature of Britain has given its Christianity a flood-based imagery. They say that our coast may have lost three miles in a thousand years. Certainly, its dwellers spent much of that time keeping the sea out. But the inlanders would not have noticed, or minded – and in many cases would never have seen the sea.

Those who lived by it were farmers and fishermen by turn. Some were marshmen, and a different breed altogether. Think of Peter Grimes. There cannot be many sea views framed in a Gothic arch as at Aldeburgh. It is how it first presents itself to the traveller to this town. The road to it once ran through the arch like a grand canopy. Or saw it as a divine approach to sea wealth or sea desolation. The great sea poet George Crabbe's severe parents lie beside it.

Like St Luke, Crabbe was a medical man and a voyager. Or, rather, the voice of those whose business was in deep waters. Both scientifically and spiritually, he took its measure. Luke's Acts of the Apostles set the lakeside faith sailing through the centuries, finding harbour here and there, but then restlessly taking to open water. The Aldeburgh fishermen meditate (chat) by their boats by the hour.

St Luke – Renaissance Man

A MODEST wind shakes the poplars in celebration of October 1987. Rooks and gulls whirl around. I am writing a sermon about St Luke and his publisher, the most excellent Theophilus, when friends arrive from Norfolk. Being still in my dressing gown, I hastily tell them about Victor Hugo writing *Les Misérables* in a cassock. They are carrying a duck casserole, strawberries, etc. (Norfolk is very classy.) Why didn't they let me know that they were coming? Although, 'Welcome, welcome.'

'But we did', and they wave a postcard to prove it. It was about to be delivered by Jamie, the postman, whom they ran into on the track.

I apologize for my scruffy state. They say that they love me as I am. I hide my tray and flourish a tablecloth, find glasses. Where did I keep my ladle? The white cat, who is a closet bohemian, dances about on a radiator. Oh, the bliss when the work routine of a writer is wrecked! They have brought enough food to last me a week. I open some nice white wine from New South Wales, where I once saw it growing. They

Forever Wormingford

are singing in a Bach or Mozart Mass, I can't quite remember which, the swift transition from bread and cheese to duck having made me mindless. What I do recall are ridiculous things such as Suffolk cheese's being so hard you could mend gates with it. We have lunch until teatime. 'You won't need to cook tonight.'

So I return to Luke. Also, I make a note to buy Hilary Mantel's terrifying novels. We met at a Lake District literature festival. She, her husband, Roger Deacon, and I, each of us with our particular writing in our faces, as it were. I went for a long walk just before I had to give my talk, and got lost, arriving on stage with not a minute to spare and wet feet. Roger went for a short swim, although it was February. Mantel sat very still in a window. Thus we momentarily see literature.

St Luke was such a good writer. Also a physician and an artist. They say that he was so many things: the anonymous walker on the Emmaus road; unmarried; St Paul's companion on the road from Troas to Philippi; and the painter of the portrait of Mary in her church in Rome. He is certainly the best travel-writer in the New Testament. But then he was free, with no family ties to hold him back, and fully creative.

We are starting an interregnum, a long space that has to be filled with our own continuities. If I added all my interregnums together, they would come to a kind of lifetime. But who is counting? The seasons pass, the apostles and saints call out their names, the altars flicker, the hymns are sung, and somebody brings a bat into the vestry. Bats are not as blind as legend would have them. Echoes guide them when they fly in darkness. When our south-aisle roof was mended, we made entrances for them. There they live according to their natural rules, and not silly human fantasies.

Forever Wormingford

One day, Isaiah says, we shall leave our idols to 'the moles and the bats'. And they will say: 'Whatever shall we do with this rubbish?' The non-natural history of the natural world still keeps many of us busy.

Tobit and Late Roses

OUR saint is Cedd, and it is his time of the year. Now and then, I take a dozen or so of us to his gaunt, gull-ridden chapel on the Essex coast to say a Saxon prayer or two, and to read Caedmon's hymn, seabirds joining in. I am fond of places that mark the beginning of all things. The chapel was built by the romantically styled Count of the Saxon Shore, but Cedd found a better use for it. Listening to Seamus Heaney reading *Beowulf* took me back there.

Cedd was an Essex boy being trained at Lindisfarne when they sent him home to make his own people Christians. He arrived by sea, and there, all cut and ready, were the Count's stones, and handy for a cathedral. Called St Peter-on-the-Wall, it is almost certainly the church that Cedd built.

The Celtic church loved sea sounds. Its song rose and fell with the waves; its mission pressed onwards like the tides. Late October for the noisy shoreline of Britain. But bring a windcheater. Meanwhile, Bottengoms Farm in its dell is still. The vine wavers. Wild duck pass in immaculate order, one bird playing sentry.

A friend scythes the orchard, and I clean out a ditch. No organist; so we sing hymns to some kind of contraption which Mike operates from the vestry. And then to harvest festival at Little Horkesley, and a perfect sermon. Part of the art of worship is to make the familiar unfamiliar. To be like

Forever Wormingford

the wind at St Peter-on-the-Wall, expected yet surprising. The white cat agrees with none of this. She likes everything to be the same for ever and ever.

Late October for Tobit. Or Micah. Micah is passionate. Tobit has a son named Tobias, who goes off with a companion who turns out to be the Archangel Raphael, no less. Moreover, Tobit has the only well-behaved dog in the Bible. The Book of Tobit was written in Greek, Latin, Syriac, Aramaic – so the Lord would have read it – and Hebrew. 'Owing to its intrinsic charm, Tobit has been one of the most popular books in the Bible.'

A young artist once visited me and said his name was Tobias, and I told him about Tobit and the angel and their dog, and how they travelled together. I forget where. Micah walked with God, distrusting friends, and is very gloomy. But an excellent author, all the same. Was it Tobit's dog that made his book a bestseller?

Gloire de Dijon roses beat against the study window as the gale gets up. Little wet pom-poms of petals. And fat buds that will never open. The melancholy of October is not to be missed. Every now and then, a shot of sun plays havoc with the sad day. I sit at my desk, saying nothing, and remember that W. H. Auden sat at his from nine to 12, whether he wrote a word or not. Then came 'cocktail time'. Writers have such strange habits. Their fingers rattle away, and so do their heads. And all else is silence.

Through the window, something shiny and scarlet catches my gaze – cherry tomatoes. And I thought I had eaten the lot! Micah grumbles because there is no cluster of grape-gleanings to eat. He needs reassurance, love. I hope that now and then he found happiness in being able to write so well. Cedd, carrying the gospel above his head, walked inland to the dark forest clearings, a travelling light. But missing the roar of the shore.

'Only Luke Is with Me'

SPORADIC rain. It has made the horses shine. But a sweet, mild morning with racing skies. Walking in this direction, the youthful John Constable, looking around, declared: 'The sky is the keynote.' He meant for the land.

Blue tits are rifling the seed-heads. But the white cat trembles – the hunt is coming through. She feels it afar off. No sound yet, but very soon the cries and yells. No comfort the lap, the study, the familiar talk. She takes to the cupboard-top, and prays to the cat gods. Then the commotion below.

Walking to collect the post, my boots clog with leaves. October is on the way out – in lovely retreat, its golds and reds blending, its warmth unlike any other warmth.

Different golds and reds in the Blue Mountains – burning colours that travel fast. How benign they were when I walked in them, their distant Sydney suburbs, how enviable. And now they are in flames. I add this disaster to the lesser ones in my petitionary prayers at matins.

But I recognize the remoteness, the natural distance from the congregation's ability to feel any true alarm. A minor crash in Colchester High Street would fright us more. Yet who can say what the bowed head is saying? Maybe a little local bad news will be giving way to some secret joy?

Trinitytide begins to draw to a close with Luke the polymath – Dr Luke, who could do anything: heal you, write like an angel, travel everywhere. I preach on Luke's zest. We're

Forever Wormingford

none of us as young as we were, and we need to hear this lively apostle. The Church's year may be petering out, but his Acts of the Apostles gets us on the road. Interestingly, he addressed it not to the Church at large, but to a single reader, Theophilus, whom he calls 'your Excellency'. This often makes me think of George Herbert placing his poems in the hands of Nicholas Ferrar.

Luke is not a storyteller in the biblical sense, but an author. We are told that he was a Gentile convert to Christianity who both spoke and wrote Greek. Not grand Greek, but marketplace Greek. It was Luke who accompanied Paul on his second and third journeys – including the memorable one via Antioch, where the words of Christ were first heard in Europe.

Luke was unmarried, and, some think, once on another road altogether – that to Emmaus. And here he is once more in the Stour Valley during his little summer. His biography is both full of facts and open to the imagination. Thus we have both a non-mythic and a non-legendary Luke; thus his collect: 'Almighty God, who calledst Luke the physician, whose praise is in the Gospel, to be an evangelist, and physician of the soul, may it please thee, that by the wholesome medicines of the doctrine delivered by him, all the diseases of our souls may be healed.'

'Only Luke is with me,' Paul would say. Only Luke! They said that his teachings contained more about prayer than any other subject. They are certainly more to our way of thinking than much of the New Testament. It is his having been so polymathic and such a good walker. Supposing they found one of his paintings in the catacombs – imagine! But we have found two of his books, thanks to the excellent Theophilus. He ran his Church with the help of women. He said that Christ was for the world, not just the Jews.

NOVEMBER

Paraclete

GULLS are so meditative. Not the greedy, noisy ones I used to see at Aldeburgh, but those on my hill field, who wheel in silence over what remains of the horse feed. This for an hour or two, then they are away. The radio speaks of a 'City of Culture'. A nonsense, really, since every city is this. How could it not be? Switch over to silence. The white cat breaks this with little cries of starvation.

A subdued November day, pleasantly empty and waiting to be filled. I take letters to David's postbox. He drove it into the orchard grass at the end of the track so as to save the postman a tidy walk. Shining mud from turning cars.

Advent is near, tremulous and as exciting as it is threatening. 'Come, thou long-expected Jesus.' Brian, master-ringer, waylays me. 'Can you take the bell-ringers' service?' Of course. When didn't I? Joanna Sturdy made two of our bells when Shakespeare was writing 'These are but wild and whirling words.'

My berryless holly hedge shines in the distance where the gale has brought down a branch of aspen; so there is much clearing-up. And some re-reading of the Advent carols – a favourite being Eleanor Farjeon's 'People, look east'. It contains a nice bird-verse, which suits my breakfast view of seagulls:

Forever Wormingford

Birds, though ye long have ceased to build,
Guard the nest that must be filled.
Even the hour when wings are frozen
He for fledging-time has chosen.
People, look East, and sing today:
Love the Bird is on the way.

The notion of the Holy Spirit becoming a bird called the Paraclete has always enchanted me. It balances on the head of the Father on the tip of the chancel at Blythburgh, as it takes off for the sea. Except, being stone, it is about to take off for ever. Frozen in its carver's art, it is Spirit solidified. As is all great sculpture.

Long ago, I sat with Henry Moore, and we talked about Turner. The debate at the time was where to put his great bequest, the suggestion then being Somerset House, and we signed a petition. But now he spreads himself in the Tate.

Henry Moore infused great masses of stone and bronze with his spirit – which is what genius alone can do. At Blythburgh, a medieval mason breathed into a lump of Barnack stone, and set it on the wing for centuries, reminding those on land and sea of the ever-flying Paraclete. A seagull must have sat for it. Or rather winged for it.

The River Blyth is estuarial here, widening from little more than a meadow-hidden stream into a broad bay, and this in turn into the North Sea itself, and in less than a dozen miles. And thus the Bird of Promise is oceanic.

Lapwings have made their annual call on what we call the lapwing field. It has been ploughed, and their iridescent greenish-white-and-black plumage is part of the November farming. They travel in flocks on rounded wings, crying sadly. The lapwing field is a port of call, and has been, maybe, since a stone bird perched on the church.

November is filled with cries and restlessness. Something is about to happen.

Kneelers

JESUS, Peter, Paul, and Stephen all knelt to pray. 'Strengthen the feeble knees,' Job prays. Now and then in scripture there are apologies for not being able to kneel down. The great novelist Henry James suffered agonies from what was lightly called writer's cramp, but when his brother William fixed him up with a typewriter – and someone who could work it – his readers were not at all pleased. Dictation had ruined his famous style. He soon found a new one, however.

But arthritis was a common hazard, and was given dismissive names – tennis elbow, the screws, etc. A craftsman from Norfolk arrived to re-lay my eighteenth-century brick floor, a large, kneeling, skilful man, who smoothed the original underlying sand and chalk tenderly before resetting the slender tiles, wiping them with a mite of wax and leaving them with little sign of generations of hobnailed boots, something that he had done since he was 15. He wore leather knee-caps. 'Yes,' he admitted, 'my knees are killing me!' Like Job, he was submissive.

People once hid occupational aches and pains for as long as they could. Anything to stay out of the workhouse. No longer able to follow his trade, John Clare's father sat on a bank, chipping stones to surface the lane.

Forever Wormingford

And now, a brilliant writer told stories to James's secretary, a young Scot who was a shorthand-typist. It was the first time that he had worked with another person sitting beside him, and with a clatter, not a noiseless nib. Visitors glance at my Olympia typewriter with alarm, and then at shelves of books with some respect. And carbons? They think of Caxton.

The leaves are sailing by at quite a rate; the November sun is warm. The white cat picks her way through the debris, and the horses discuss the climate on the hill. None of these animals have done a day's work in their lives. Now and then, they are engulfed in gulls. I am engulfed in digging up a little apple-tree from where it has seeded itself by the front door, to put it in the orchard. I rock it gently, loosening its roots. Like us, plants must breathe and grow. Inside, the dreaded filing awaits. Oh, for James's saviour. I remember an ancient joke: the typist returns with the letter and tells her boss: 'I couldn't spell psychology; so I drew it.'

A talk on the radio accidentally chimes with James. I am back in New York with the London plane-leaves whirling by, and the windy city is 'blowing your head off'. It is one of the world's best walking cities where one can step it out. Life, that is. It is mathematical. No wonder Americans find European towns bewildering and illogical. And the way in which we prop up clearly done-for old buildings instead of pulling them down! They shake their heads. Just imagine what London would look like had it not been for the great fire.

At this moment, I am thinking of what it looks like now, particularly in the parks, on this lovely November morning, and from the top of a bus, maybe. Lunch on the steps of

Forever Wormingford

St Paul's. Evensong for the few at four. Golden Bath stone, townie pigeons, the Thames a Turner.

Writers are often allowed a memory like a haversack, a pile of unsorted experiences from which they can pull out something to suit the day. We are asked to remember William Temple. Short-lived, alas. St Leonard, too, who was a hermit. These lives flutter in my head and need anchorage. In our churchyard, the stripped trees are rooted in the dead, but full of life.

Ash before Oak

SOMEBODY has sent me Cerrini's *Head of Goliath*, on a postcard from Rome. The giant-killer is beautiful, and the head is appalling. A shepherd's sling and the giant's sword lie on the ground. David looks up to heaven, and poor Goliath to the earth. I say poor Goliath, because he has always seemed to me someone who is too tall for his own good.

And yet he was only about six-and-a-half feet tall. Judging by the size of his head, he would have had to be at least 20 feet in his sandals. He came from Gath, the home of another big man, Samson. Immediately after David's slaughter of Goliath, with a pebble from the brook, Prince Jonathan met David, and fell in love with him. The shepherd lad, being the greatest poet in the Bible, was able to cure Jonathan's father of his fits of depression.

The books of Samuel and Kings were Thomas Hardy's favourite reading. They contained his most loved words: 'But the Lord was not in the wind: and after the wind an earthquake; but the Lord was not in the earthquake: and after the

Forever Wormingford

earthquake a fire; but the Lord was not in the fire: and after the fire a still small voice.'

They are on his memorial window in Stinsford Church. Or, if you read the New English: 'And after the fire a low murmuring sound', which is not quite right, and makes one think of inarticulate noise in E. M. Forster's cave. You see how one's mind wanders.

Meanwhile, the November morning smiles. All the ash leaves have fallen down, but the oak leaves will hang on until Christmas. White gulls are black in the distance. People call. The white cat ignores them. Bird feeders hang from the old rose, and are obscured by blue tits and chaffinches. I write the Remembrance Day service, then clear up the tumbling willow.

I think of my friend Richard Birt, in far-off Hereford, who, to my mind, has done more to bring Thomas Traherne back into mind than anyone else. In fact, my head goes here and there, as is its wont, being governed by words.

Visitors gather sloes. What a sensation they were when we were children, as we gathered up our daring palette. 'Where do you pick your sloes?' We would pass a needle through them, and drown them in gin. The first taste lasts a lifetime for country people.

Snowy gliders pass silently over the house. Americans holler and shout on the radio. I pray for poor dear New York, and all the drowned East Coast. I remember the London plane trees in Manhattan Central Park, and the way their leaves bowled along the sidewalk, and now lie in sodden masses. It is unutterably sad. I suppose that most American men are taller than Goliath.

Forever Wormingford

But I must cease this drifting, and pull my mind together. Searching for something else, a postcard of Rupert Brooke's grave in Skyros tumbles from a book. To the early hero-seekers of the First World War, he was a David. His body lies under massive protection. Stone and iron keep it out of reach. A mosquito killed him on the way to the Dardanelles, where, at that moment, my teenage father was also sailing, but in another troop ship.

Poor straws! on the dark flood we catch awhile,
Cling, and are borne into the night apart.

George Herbert and the Backs

I AM in Cambridge, and far from home. Drizzle marks my path. Peter and I stare at signatures in the university library, chat to young folk who are making their way in the world, and, eventually, take our places at high table. I talk alternately to an American lady from Maine and the Bishop of Ely.

For no reason whatsoever, I find myself thinking about George Herbert's petition to the government on the small matter of not draining the fens. He – everyone – although coughing their lives away, are more concerned with retaining the loveliness of the Backs than losing their health. Herbert thanks King James for securing the waters over which the Muses delight to reign.

'That river, on the banks of which . . . flows through our college gardens, and strews flowers all around, is of far higher value than all the swamps and morasses in the land.' And thus the 'fen ague' fed on his lungs, and those of countless others; so that coughing drowned out the lute music. But

Forever Wormingford

although King James might easily be persuaded to grant the petitions of young Mr Herbert, his Secretary of State could not, and soon a whole new climate emerged, and the choking and spitting would stop. 'Love and a cough cannot be hid' became one of Herbert's favourite proverbs.

The Bishop and I imagined pre-drained Ely – the Isle of Eels, and its mighty prelates. Those were the days. Then a rumour ran round the table. No women bishops . . . It was like the way in which rumour struck at happiness long ago, altering the day.

We arrived home late at night. The white cat lay full length on a laburnum, oak leaves whirling round her. She was looking not best pleased. My old white house gleamed ahead, waiting to be entered. The blooms on the John Clare rose were black in the night. The garden light wavered in the vine.

Shocked when Herbert asked for humble Bemerton, all tumbledown and unworthy of a gentleman, they added tumbledown Leighton Bromswold, in Huntingdonshire. To his mother's horror, he mended them both, making the aisle at Leighton especially wide to fit Isaiah's prophecy. 'And a highway shall be there, and a way, and it shall be called the way of holiness, the unclean shall not pass over it, but it shall be for those, the wayfaring men . . . and the redeemed shall walk there.' It is the conclusion of Isaiah 35, the chapter which begins with the enchanting words, 'The wilderness and the solitary place shall be glad for them, and the desert shall rejoice and blossom as the rose.'

Herbert adored these words. He loved the word 'Temple', and the proverb 'Building is sweet impoverishment.' He clasped the chalky, sweeping, secretly intended, airy, ancient spread of Wiltshire to him with the rapture of another consumptive, Richard Jefferies, who was also 39 when he died.

Forever Wormingford

Herbert thought that God had given us two paradises – one on earth, one in heaven. And that with the blessed playfulness of his 'King'. They would walk and ride together, chatting away. His mother shook her head. But then she always laid a place for Christ at her table. So what could one say? He encouraged one to take liberties.

Squirrels are hogging the bird seed. Rain falls fast. Clouds race at a fair spit. Books rock about, and must be put in their place.

DECEMBER

St Edmund's Day

TORRENTIAL rain for St Edmund, our Sebastian-like protector, his cult a thousand years old. Thin and shiny on his plinth, bristling with arrows, he watches us process by under our umbrellas as we hurry into the dry.

Legend has it that he was 15 when they crowned him King of the Angles on Christmas Day on the height opposite my bedroom, this being the borderland of the East Angles and the East Saxons – a German prince who had inherited the crown. For many years, he was our patron saint. Then the crusaders changed him for a soldier – St George. Some would change George for Edmund at this moment, but when one is old, one tends to make do with existing arrangements, all passion being spent.

Frances Ward and Janet Wheeler are less feeble, and have presented us with a fiery anthem in which holy Edmund's decapitation, horribly reminiscent of what has been occurring at this moment, makes him a shockingly contemporary Christian. There is no escaping the darkness of every age.

Time was when history in church was a local tableau staged by children. Now, it is terribly grown-up. Bronze St Edmund on his plinth in the pouring rain is the young man who leaves England for Syria to 'help out', and is murdered for his pains. Time was when days like this were country pageantry; now, they stage human history of the moment, and it can be terrible.

Forever Wormingford

No peasants today, only mayors in tricorne hats and golden chains, a Lord Lieutenant, the higher clergy, bell-ringers, and the dear familiar faces of those who make great churches spotless, who launder, brush, polish, arrange flowers, mend, lay markers in huge books, carry processional crosses, hand out this and that, and keep the rich interior movement going. And trumpeters for Britten's *Fanfare*. And then Marriott's oceanic plea for wisdom, love, and might to 'move o'er the water's face'.

I fancied that I could hear the rain bouncing on the leads and the gargoyles' guiding it to the ground. Old churches take the local climate in hand, splashing it away from their walls, channelling it into graves and beneath huge trees. The distant sound of it accompanies the anthem, a Beowulfian hymn by the Dean and her friend, a confrontation of the barbaric and the Christian. That continuous war of opposites in which nothing seems to change whatever the century.

Christ is revealed, but so is human enormity. Hope looks on. Robert Bridges echoes Christ's sad prophecy on the Jerusalem Temple, then brand new. When George Herbert died, they called his poems *The Temple*. He called them 'my writings'. But the Church of England sees its language architecturally, building up its faith to dizzy heights and allowing it to sink to depths from which it has to be rescued.

On St Edmund's Day, everything is said, sung, and done to the sound of the rain – a steady autumnal downpour that finds out where roofs are fragile, and roads are sinking. Our car has to nose its way through it, like an ark pointed towards a haven, its windscreen wipers like a metronome. Or a pulse.

We travel through a hurricane, but when we brake and stop, it is hardly raining at all. It is not quite light when I look for Edmund's coronation hill over the Stour. It is, at usual, no more than a watercolour brush-stroke; a barely visible sign that he was there. And thus here with us still.

The Unremembered Ones

JUST up the lane, children are snatching at breakfast, and grown-ups are snatching at time. But I am looking out of the window, as usual, and musing on birds; just as R. S. Thomas did, when he walked to the Llyn peninsula to give them a piece of his mind.

It was an uncompromising mind: God-questioning, restless, brilliant in patches, and, while thoroughly Franciscan, not at ease. Like my seagulls at this moment. White and impatient, they whirl around Duncan's field. How black they are on the wing, how snowy when they land. And how angelic. They remind me of Francis Thompson when he said: 'The angels keep their ancient places; Turn but a stone, and start a wing!'

The gull's wing on the kitchen table has started these thoughts. I cannot bear to think of how it has landed there. It is pure and perfect, yet mutilated. A friend took it out of her bag and left it there. I put it on a shelf, and then in a rose bed. I think of wooden wings in Suffolk churches – the ones that the reformers tried to shoot down, but only succeeded in winging. So they continue to fly to us from the Middle Ages, some of them nesting in Blythburgh to hold up the manorial claims of our gentry.

My gull's wing is a far cry from all this. When we were children, we wondered when wings would sprout from our skinny shoulder-blades. Much later, as a fanciful grown-up flying to Sydney, I would meditate on the thinness of the plane floor that cut me off from the earth. Neither angels nor gulls flew past this window, only nameless cities, miles below. Coffee was served. A novel spoke of love.

But today my feet are very much on the ground, because I am raking up autumn leaves. All around there is a haunting autumn quiet and a ghostly December mist, a great yellowing and nature's terminal beauty. Ash leaves actually tumble down on to my head, like the sad artificial poppies in the Royal Albert Hall a fortnight ago.

The Prayer Book lists names for the boy who will soon be born. They are very grand, but his name is Jesus, his carpenter father says. There is a Staffordshire figure of the three of them – Joseph, Mary, and their child – on the farmhouse mantelpiece, on the run to Egypt: father carrying his tools; Mary seated on an ass, clasping her baby; Joseph walking. The everlasting refugees.

These ornaments were 'fairings', something you won on coconut-shies. Rural treasures which saw the generations out. I must wash it for Christmas. In church, I must remember to repeat the first collect throughout Advent, the one that promises us to rise to immortality. The one that is perfect liturgy and theology. The one in which we put on the armour of light, rising white like the gulls.

The Christmas shopping-list begins with a new scythe, the old one having got crooked in the wrong way. I must be the only person in my circle who is able to swing one. Passers-by watch me nervously. Never mind, one can do with a bit of awe. The withering orchard grass falls before it, sowing next year's seeds on the way. A somnolence attends everything, but next summer's flowers are counting the days.

Forever Wormingford

Christmas shopping battles away in the country towns — although people are hard-up, they say. I think of the oaks and ashes that were felled to make angels.

School Bus

EACH December, I wander about the town in search of the charity-card shop, this time as I come, reassured, from the dentist. And there it is, with a lady sweeping its pavement, and its racks of greetings and fearful diseases, snowy churches, and Renaissance nativities. And there, as usual, is my baptismal Suffolk church, covered in drift — only serendipitously 'different'.

Looking for a familiar scene, I find, centre-stage, Great Aunt Agnes's and Uncle Fred's gravestones. He had died early from Western Front gas. She had been low in our estimation, feeding us with bread and butter instead of cake when we called after a three-mile hike through the prickly cornfields.

Her house was a clapboard wonder. We stepped down into it when we called. Remote faces from the trenches stared at us as we parked, good as gold, on her slippery couch as she sawed away at a home-made loaf, holding it against her stout body. But here she is, in the charity-card shop, next to good-looking — they always said — Fred. I bought two packs.

The white cat mutters at birds. She has come inside until the spring. Bullfinches and robins whirl around the new feeder. The farm track has stopped being a river. Washed sparkling clean, it dries out in a cloudy sun. I take a memorial service for a neighbour in a packed church. 'Afterwards in the village hall'. And so it goes on. Life. And just as it always did. For, as Ludwig Wittgenstein said, 'Resting on your laurels is

Forever Wormingford

as dangerous as resting when you are walking in snow. You doze off and die in your sleep.'

Having finished a new book, may I not rest? 'At rest' was the popular epitaph in a country churchyard. How they toiled! Now they 'sleep'. And so soundly that Barry's mower never wakes them up. I trust that my ashes won't 'sleep'. I run my eyes over their trunks apprehensively. So far, so smooth. So alive! Even in December.

I cast away the old lectionary. It is my first Advent gesture. Whom have we here? Anyone know? Ambrose, Nicholas Ferrar, John of Damascus, Mary . . . with child? We sing the Advent hymns, sonorous with titles. 'Come, thou long-expected Jesus.' I begin the clearance of sodden leaves – and find patches of pink cyclamen. Dead sticks have rattled down. Late roses have pushed through the guttering. Last year's Christmas puddings have made their presence known.

Shopping on the eight-o'clock school bus, how different things are! What used to be a zoo on wheels is now part silence, part murmur. Forty or so teenagers. Pairs of lovers, solitary dreamers, youngsters giving nothing away but simply travelling – like the boy in Thomas Hardy's poem with the train ticket in his hat. At Bures Hamlet, buses from opposite directions have to squeeze between the banks, and people who are reading look up.

I rode on these buses when I was 12. When we passed the Treble Tile pub, the conductor would call out 'the Terrible Tile' and laugh at his wit. Everyone smoked. We rode in a travelling ashtray. But the views are exactly the same. And we still say 'Thank you' to the driver as we get off. He calls me Sir. Old women call him Dear. I read Patrick Leigh Fermor's *The Traveller's Tree*, careful not to forget my stop.

Forever Wormingford
Poverty

THE Christmas-card snowstorm brings in an atlas of my life. Views of every parish I have been to: familiar parishes, glimpsed parishes, parishes I have worked in, parishes in which I have felt the presence of artists and writers. And priests, of course. And naturalists. And those adopted by retired friends.

Long ago (for I doubt if the courtesy is still observed) an incumbent would offer his successor the convention of moving at least five miles away, so as not to get in his hair, so to speak – although, once addressing the retired clergy of East Anglia, I was aware that it is often during the final years of ministry that a priest and his wife, or her husband, are apt to make their most important friends.

I have been in Wormingford, on and off, since I was 22 – first of all as the friend of the artists John and Christine Nash, and later as the dweller in their remote farmhouse. My feet have kept the track to it open, if not level, and the view from it familiar.

On this near-Christmas day, I stare from its high north window, just as John once stared from it when he placed a canvas on his easel every week, and, cigarette between teeth, would transfer sketchbook drawings to oils.

The studio in those guiltless days was a homily to dust. Tobacco dust, mortal dust from plants and insects, and, to a degree, from the artist himself. It was never swept, and a single 40-watt bulb gave a discreet account of it.

During the summer, when John went to Cornwall or Scotland (never abroad, if he could help it), he would kindly dust a patch where I could write. I never told him that I never wrote a word in his studio, but always in his lovely garden; for summer went on for ever at Bottengoms. Still does. Even at this moment, with Christmas at my heel, the valley within a valley which contains the old house has its own climate. Should it snow, everyone knows that I won't be able to get to the top. The dip will fill up, hedges will disappear, familiar posts will vanish, and ditches will sound with loud but invisible water. Only no one could imagine such a sinking out of sight today, and the postman's van flies towards me with a flourish, and yesterday's cleared desk hides under the avalanche.

Few birds sing, but a squirrel scuttles in the roof, and the white cat is torpid. The News creates a strange unease. People are going to foodbanks. Dickensian activity on cards is one thing, in twenty-first-century Britain, quite another. The poverty of the Holy Family resumes its traditional reality, and is no longer an old tale. All but the well-off would have had no difficulty in identifying with it since Christianity began. In our day, just now and then, it became academic, and below the surface of our time, but it never went away. It was always there, the fragility of human life, and in our world, not the Third World. With the poor and meek and lowly lived on earth our Saviour holy. It was and is true. Politics fail, especially in winter, and spectacularly at Christmas.

Yet the divine birthday is here again, and its light contains no variableness, neither shadow of turning. It is the perfect gift for Christmas. We should see by it. It exists for this purpose. Comprehending our childishness, it tolerates the tinsel. We are young now, whatever age we are.

Forever Wormingford
The Holly Hedge

JOURNALISTS are proud of what they call 'rolling news'. But I am flattened by it. Thus this past two weeks in particular I have rationed its horrors, one blanched young father's face on the screen making it unnecessary to hear anything more.

I read the collect for Holy Innocents' Day at matins, but did not add my ha'p'orth of sympathy in the sermon. Rage, really. That such things should happen.

Quietness at dawn put the news in its place. The Gospel for this day is the flight into Egypt: 'Arise, and take the young child and his mother,' God tells Joseph, 'and flee into Egypt, and be thou there until I bring thee word.' A clumsy pottery image of this event stands on the old kitchen shelf. It is what was called a 'fairing', i.e. a Victorian prize won at a coconut-shy. The Virgin rides; the father walks.

On the screen, the driven-from-home Syrian boys and girls, in thin cotton clothes, burn cardboard to keep warm. The conclusion of the Innocents' Day Gospel is unbearable; yet there cannot be a better lament for what I witness far off. 'In Rama was there a voice heard, lamentation, and weeping, and great mourning, Rachel weeping for her children, and would not be comforted, because they are not.'

It is mild. Springlike, even. Primroses bloom between the paving stones, and chaffinches bounce around in the crumbs. Streaky morning skies; the white cat's putting out a dark paw to test the temperature. I write out two Nine Lessons and Carols, one for Mount Bures, one for here. A farmer, a bell-ringer, a commuter, on I go. The aisles glitter, and smell of pine needles. All is well. The crib flickers. 'Thanks be to God.' Mulled wine. All this ritual worn to a frazzle by its annual repetition; yet it shines.

Forever Wormingford

Joachim will be on his way from Berlin, with its Baltic cold, and Ian on his way from Norfolk, which could be windy. I must rake a path to the house as invitingly as possible. And bring in holly from the vast hedge. What does my old friend Richard Mabey say about this shiny plant? A huge amount.

Ilex aquifolium. Or hollin. A practical mystical tree. My neighbour will be making holly wreaths for the churchyard and front doors. I crown the oak post that holds up the entrance hall with it. Log fires will shrivel its leaves long before Twelfth Night. But holly trees will be left in the field-hedges for ploughing marks, although the dozen shares on Tom's plough monster, guided by remote control, have long done with them. Yet a reverence, even a fear, of holly, will guarantee its survival.

My holly hedge was reasonable enough 40 years ago, but now it scrapes the sky. Whippy thin boughs stretch from it in order to flourish. Few berries. The hedge needs a good trim.

It was planted maybe centuries ago, as part of the old garden hedge, to keep the stock from getting at the vegetables, but now its only use is Christmas. The wreath-makers carry it about in sacks. Their fingers are torn and reddened. It is surprising how, at Christmas, the hands of so many villagers become the hands of their ancestors, owing to holly.

I see these wounded hands at the communion rail. They take the chalice that was in use when Shakespeare was writing *Twelfth Night*, cuddling it carefully, candlelight on their hair. I don't like the way that these ancient cups, from which generations of parishioners have taken the sacrament, are put into cathedral museums. Some time ago, the cup that George Herbert used at Bemerton was kindly brought from

Forever Wormingford

Salisbury Cathedral for me to use – and has since permanently shed its glass case.

For Herbert, Christmas was for singing. He was a fine lutenist, and I like to imagine him singing in Bemerton Church at maybe the only two Christmases he spent there before death silenced him.

> The shepherds sing: and shall I silent be?
> My God, no hymn for thee?
> My soul's a shepherd too; a flock it feeds
> Of thoughts and words, and deeds.

He goes on to see each of us as Christmas candles, 'a willing shiner':

> Then we will sing, shine all our own day,
> And one another pay:
> His beams shall cheer my breast, and both so twine,
> Till ev'n his beams sing, and my musick shine.

Herbert was at an inn, and not in church when he wrote this poem. An inn on Christmas Day: a country pub with people singing. And Christ singing alongside them. The poet adored his Lord in church, but almost preferred meeting him in his rectory, the Salisbury lanes, the Wiltshire fields. Jesus and music – and conversation – all came together in such places, naturally and intimately. And, since Herbert knew that his life here would be brief, he knew, too, that he must make the most of it, riding in the fresh air with his perfect friend – who, no doubt, was singing, too.

Forever Wormingford
Carols

I AM writing our Nine Lessons and Carols. The mid-Advent sun blazes through the study window, and is hot on my back. The white cat dreams on a radiator. Chaffinches swing on the feeder. I write Churchwarden, Bell-ringer, Boy, Commuter, Girl, Farmer, Mother, Gardener, Lay Canon. Then I read the incomparable *Oxford Book of Carols*, and, as always, mourn our limitation.

Percy Dearmer, Ralph Vaughan Williams, and Martin Shaw edited this masterpiece in 1928. Here are 200 carols, plus a preface and notes, the latter as intoxicating as honey-wine, shall we say. Once upon a time, *carola* meant a dancing choir. Try that at King's. The clergy were anti-carol for ages.

'Please, Sir, may we sing a carol?' the people asked Parson Woodforde on Christmas morning.

'Yes, but wait until I am out of the church.'

This in 1788.

It was Percy Dearmer who wrote the fine essay on carols in my treasured collection. He was the Vicar of St Mary's, Primrose Hill, and Professor of Ecclesiastical Art at King's College, London.

> Omega and Alpha he!
> Let the organ thunder,
> While the choir with peals of glee
> Doth rend the air asunder.

There were giants in church in those days. Meanwhile, I sort out small gifts. How can I thank Jamie the postman for

Forever Wormingford

bumping down the ancient track every mid-morning without fail? Or the unseen milkman? Or the saintly ones who drive me to services? Or the day for breaking, and the midnight frost for glittering? Or Advent for being so thrilling?

Dearmer wrote:

Perhaps nothing is just now of such importance [it was the early post-First World War aftermath] as to increase the element of joy in religion; people crowd in our churches at the Christmas, Easter, and Harvest Festivals, largely because the hymns for those occasions are full of a sound hilarity; if carol books were in continual use [there are carols for every season], that most Christian and most forgotten element would be vastly increased, in some of its loveliest forms, all through the year.

In the high street, two lads play Bach to the taxi rank. Children stare up at them in wonder. A few steps away is the big old house in which John Wilbye played the lute when Shakespeare was alive, his wage the lease on a sheep farm. Both of them would have sung a carol called 'The Song of the Ship' for Advent.

There comes a ship
– sailing,
With angels flying fast;
She bears a splendid cargo
And has a mighty mast.
This ship is fully laden,
Right to her highest board,

Forever Wormingford

She bears the son from Heaven,
God's high eternal Word.

Christmas in Cornwall

NOT a madeleine, but a pale-yellow spotty apple from a Cornish garden. A fat cooker that no self-regarding supermarket would stock, but which, for me, belongs to the epulae (feast) shelf. A poet friend, James Turner, planted this apple long ago, made this garden, hid it behind a five-barred gate, and allowed me to weed it.

Eventually, his ancient home fell into later hands, those of an artist, and she has brought me this evocative Christmas present. I core it, run a sharp knife round its girth, pack it with raisins, and, oh golly, what a rush back over the years to the Cornish Christmases.

I would leave Suffolk at dawn, get to Paddington, make sure to be on the left side of the carriage so as not to miss the red desiccated rocks at Dawlish, and arrive at Bodmin Road in the early evening. The poet and his wife would then emerge from their little car in their duffel coats, show muted gratitude for my brace of Suffolk pheasants, brag about the eternal spring of the Cornish climate, and carry me off to the lovely house in the watery valley.

Their neighbours were an outspoken old lady who sold camomile plants to make camomile lawns, a silent old man who read ten library books a week, and some wildish dogs. Their house stood next to what might have been a medieval cell for a monk or two.

Forever Wormingford

On Christmas morning, James and I drove to the eight-o'clock in a bitterly cold church, where he would purposely kneel on the damp stone floor, and I would carefully balance on a big stuffed hassock. The communicants dotted themselves around the nave, and our prayerful breath left our lips in little clouds.

In the churchyard, the dead crowded each other in their shiny slate graves. But we – the worshippers – were careful to space ourselves out so as not to cry 'Happy Christmas!' Then home to an enormous breakfast. And an enormous lunch-cum-dinner; for it seemed to go on all day. And talk by the blazing logs – mostly, where James was concerned, about the iniquity and folly of publishers. And, on Boxing Day, the long walk along Constantine Bay, where, contrary to church, we yelled at everyone we met.

James's friends included Charles Causley. The three of us would be in a more accepting mood where publishers were concerned as we drank bitter in the pub. Charles was dry and merry, and had just been given the Queen's Gold Medal for Poetry. When he gave me his books, he would change a line here and there with his fountain pen. There were other writers, too, for literature is usually made up of small gatherings in scraps of landscape. Charles knew eastern England; for he had had his teacher-training there, but his epicentre was, of course, Launceston, where he was on speaking terms with every cat.

Three more Treneague cookers to come; three more evocations of the Cornish Christmases and their winter guests. Blowy drives to the Cheesewring on Bodmin Moor. Searches for Thomas Hardy at Boscastle. The weather always a bit

Forever Wormingford

wet. Never-ending drinks with friends on clifftops: 'Don't go, don't go.' Shy glimpses of John Betjeman at Daymer Bay, and later to his grave by the church, which his father had rescued from the sand, once to find rabbits dining on it.

And always, surprisingly, wild flowers in bloom without a winter break.